FEAST and FAMINE

D.S. HALACY, Jr.

MACRAE SMITH COMPANY · *Philadelphia*

ST. PHILIPS COLLEGE LIBRARY

Copyright © 1971 by D.S. Halacy, Jr.

All rights reserved. No part of this book may be reproduced in any form without permission in writing from the publisher, except by a reviewer, who may quote brief passages in a review to be printed in a magazine or newspaper.

ISBN: 0-8255-4031-3

Library of Congress Catalog Card Number 78-150677

Manufactured in the United States of America
Published simultaneously in Canada by
George J. McLeod, Limited, Toronto.

7109

The author and publisher thank the United Nations Food and Agricultural Organization for use of the many photographs throughout the book identified by the initials "FAO."

SECOND PRINTING

Contents

MAN AND FOOD

1 The Need for Food 1

2 The Great Food Chain 15

3 Converting Food and Energy 29

4 The Basic Foodstuffs 42

5 Meat: A Luxury Food? 57

6 The Agricultural Revolution 70

7 Food—Our Largest Industry 87

8 The Problems of Pollution 107

9 Our Exploding Population 123

10 To Feed the World 138

Index 156

CHAPTER 1

The Need for Food

> Millions of people in Asia, Africa, and Latin America go to bed every night wondering whether they will have enough food the next day to keep them alive. Millions of people in the United States go to bed every night wondering whether they will have enough will power the next day to keep them on their low-calorie diets.
>
> W. Barr, *Nutrition, A World Concern*

What is the number one industry in the United States? Steelmaking, automobiles, home building? None of these is the answer. The largest single industry in our country, as in all the world, is food. In the United States alone we spend more than $75 billion each year to keep ourselves well fed. Too well fed, in fact, for perhaps more of us eat too much than too little. Three times each day we spend from fifteen minutes to an hour in the process of eating. Not quite as ingrained a habit as breathing, eating is basic to living. We don't eat just because we enjoy food, although that enjoyment makes the process much pleasanter than it must be for those who have no appetite. Although some unfortunates among us live to eat—or at least give that impression at the table—we eat to live.

FOOD, THE HUMAN FUEL

Ancient physicians were well aware of the importance of food, and the great Hippocrates, "father of medicine," urged moderation in diet for his patients. To him is also attributed the well-known saying "One man's meat is another's poison." In particular, he understood the purpose of food as fuel. "Growing bodies have the most innate heat," said Hippocrates.

The top of the food pyramid: A family shops for packaged food American-style, at a self-service market. U.S. Department of Agriculture Photo.

"They therefore require the most food, for otherwise their bodies are wasted. In old persons, the heat is feeble, and therefore they require little fuel, as it were, to the flame, for it would be extinguished by much."

Another Greek physician, Galen, born in 130 A.D., about 500 years after Hippocrates, also set down in his *Opera Omnia* a very clear picture of food as fuel:

> Just as the proper nutriment for fire increases it, in the same manner nutriment that is proper and natural for bodies warm by nature will always strengthen them and increase their inborn heat. And this is the property of all food. Sometimes, however, too much food weakens the innate heat, after the manner of wet wood. For this too is nutriment for the fire, but if heaped on the

fire it is too much and therefore conceals the flame and threatens extinction.

While we cannot live on petroleum or wood, humans are actually much less finicky about fuel than engines are. There are hundreds of different foods, and diets vary not only from country to country but from state to state and even from city to city. Fortunately, there is a broad choice available, so that generally we can each find something we enjoy while it is providing nourishment for us.

Eating is more or less automatic with us. Only when we miss a meal or are forced to wait a long time between meals are we reminded that without food we get hungry. Hunger, the pangs in our stomach and the craving in our minds for a thick steak or a big dish of vegetables, is nature's method of assuring our bodies an ample supply of fuel to provide the energy we use in everyday living. Driving a car fifteen miles may require about a gallon of gasoline containing 26,000 *calories* of heat energy. To walk that far, one's body requires a certain number of calories too.

The word calorie, so well known in connection with diets and nutrition, comes from *calor*, a Latin word meaning heat. Let's be sure what we mean by a calorie. Webster defines calorie as "the amount of heat required at a pressure of one atmosphere to raise the temperature of one gram of water one degree centigrade."

This unit is more accurately called a *gram-calorie*. One gram of water is only a good-sized drop, since it is a cubic centimeter, less than half an inch on a side. A gram-calorie doesn't go far, either as engine fuel or food, so engineers and nutritionists alike use the term "kilogram-calorie" or "kilocalorie," a quantity of heat energy one thousand times that of a gram-calorie. When you go on a diet of 2000 calories a day it is really two *million* gram-calories. These 2000 kilocalories of food contain enough energy to heat five gallons of water from zero degrees to boiling. To cook our food, we use a fair fraction of as much energy as there is in it. But we humans consume far less energy than our automobiles because we are "fractional-horsepower" (about one eighth) engines in comparison with our many-horsepower automobiles.

A single pint of gasoline contains enough heat energy to fuel a human for a day, although of course it is not in a form we can use. A hamburger is equivalent in energy to two ounces of gasoline, a quart of orange juice matches a pound of coal, and a fair-sized piece of candy has as much energy as a stick of dynamite! Fortunately the candy does not give up its energy as explosively as the dynamite, but the energy is there nevertheless.

About 10½ kilogram-calories per minute are required to produce one horsepower. Thus our average 3000-calorie-a-day diet would produce one horsepower for about five hours if the human body were 100 percent efficient, which it is not. We do not need to produce as much power as a horse, but most of the energy we get from food does go for physical labor such as walking, running, lifting, throwing, digging, and climbing. An athlete or laborer requires more food energy than one who sits all day at a desk, and a large person requires more food than a small one.

All our food energy is not for physical movement. Unlike a machine, our bodies are made of living cells, and the cells themselves need energy to function, in addition to our requirements of heat to keep us warm and energy to keep us going. When we are young, a good part of our food intake goes to make cells grow so that our bodies as a whole can grow too.

LIVING TO EAT

Historically, man has never had enough to eat. To be sure, in some cases individuals had temporary oversupplies and stuffed themselves against the day when there would be no food at all. But in general, man's food problem was finding enough to eat and eating all he found. Today, in our part of the world, there is increasing danger in the other direction—the danger of eating too much.

As is shockingly portrayed in some of the paintings of Pieter Breughel, even in seventeenth-century Europe there was gluttonous high living side by side with starvation. Only in the last century has this been generally true, however, and there are still, tragically, a great many people dying each day of starvation or the effects of malnutrition. However, overweight is a bigger problem in the United States and in many other developed or advanced countries. It is almost as though nature has never been faced with this problem before and has trained us to eat everything in sight! The result is that diet foods are big business in our country.

While there are cases of obesity caused by body chemistry out of control, for much of our fat we really have no excuse except uncontrolled appetites. Children are often brought up in an environment that encourages plumpness as an indication of health and well-being. Some nutritionists believe that when young people overeat, physiological changes take place so that their body cells crave an excess of food for the rest of their lives. In other words, they must keep feeding the mountains of fat they created early in life.

There are some fortunate individuals who seemingly without conscious effort stay trim and healthy with regard to weight. In their case, the body's automatic sensing equipment is operating at high efficiency. With little or no dieting as such, they control their intake so that it matches the expenditure of food energy.

Another change in our habits further complicates the picture. Although we may think that we labor strenuously, most of us today do not work as hard physically as did our ancestors. Natural evolution is a far slower process than technological change; nature still has not gotten the message that man is relying on engines and motors to do work he once did himself with muscle power.

FOOD CAN KILL

Nature's storage of fat in the body is a built-in safeguard against starvation. The location of the treasure-houses of stored food are not only obvious but the source of jokes and ridicule as well. In ancient times men often went without food for days because there was no food available, and their bodies lived off the stored fats. Today in our country, and in many other places, this stored fat not only is not burned away periodically but is continually added to.

What is overweight? Certainly we should not each of us weigh exactly the same for the same height and age. This would lead to a rather regimented physical appearance and no regard for differences in build. A variation of a few pounds either way is no cause for a crash diet to lose *or* gain. From 10 to 20 percent above normal is considered overweight, however. More than 20 percent overweight is termed obese. Tragically, about a third of us in the United States are obese. And the great majority of us are overweight to some degree.

Let's start with a normal-weight person, assuming that his longevity is normal and his risk of disease is normal. If we add 10 percent to his weight, what happens? It would be bad enough if his life was endangered by even that much, but the price we pay for overindulgence is even higher.

Statistics from insurance companies, who have the facts of life *and* death, show that 10 percent overweight means 13 percent greater likelihood of dying. Increase the overweight to 20 percent and the risk jumps to 25 percent. And at 30 percent overweight the figure of risk goes to 42 percent. While these figures are for men, women too are endangered severely by overweight conditions, with increased death rates almost exactly matching the percentage of overweight.

Few people die of overeating in a direct sense. But so do few people die from outright starvation. Most hunger deaths come from malnutrition, or poor food, rather than no food at all. Many more die from diseases brought on or aggravated by malnutrition than from lack of food quantity or quality itself. In a similar way overeating is a contributor to many deaths in the developed countries, particularly Western Germany, North America, and other places where there is an abundance of both money and food.

Heart trouble is the commonest cause of food-related deaths and illnesses. There are two basic reasons. First, excess weight puts a heavy physical strain on the heart. The exertion necessary to move an extra fifty pounds overtaxes an organ never designed for such abuse. Second, overeating of fats and dairy products can cause atherosclerosis, a form of hardening of the arteries that leads to strokes or heart attacks.

Diseases of the heart and circulatory system are not the only results of overeating. Overeating also overworks the kidneys, which have the task of eliminating wastes and poisons from the body. It is also thought that overweight persons tend to have diabetes. The United States Department of Agriculture mentions these diseases as caused by overeating, and adds also hypertension, cerebral strokes, and cancer. Thus, while diet is not responsible for as many diseases as some people fear, it is most important to our health, and too much food can be as dangerous as too little. How ironic for millions to be dying of too much food instead of too little!

Medical missionaries among the Eskimos have compiled a long list of diseases the white man conferred on these people by changing their high-meat, high-fat diet to that of modern civilization:

arthritis	gallstones
appendicitis	gastric ulcers
beriberi	hypertension
cancer	night blindness

The Need for Food • 7

dental decay
constipation
corpulence
diabetes
epilepsy

pellagra
ricketts
rheumatism
scurvy

Heart disease seems to be the most deadly of those caused by food. As a result there has recently been a great furore over the significance of cholesterol in the diet, and the impression is general that this is a new discovery by nutritionists. However, the fact that cholesterol caused fatty deposits in the arteries was made by a Russian doctor named Amitschow in 1913. Conflicting results and theories kept the anti-cholesterol idea from making any headway until some forty years later.

Cholesterol is one of many "steroids," or biologically active organic compounds, in the body. Hormones are steroids, as are some forms of vitamin D, cortisone, and digitalis. A number of body tissues synthesize cholesterol, but most of it is manufactured in the liver. It is interesting that cholesterol comprises 14 percent of the white matter of the brain and 6 percent of the gray matter. However, the heart and its circulatory system normally contain only a fraction of one percent of cholesterol. All the major classes of foodstuffs, carbohydrates, fats, and protein, can be converted into cholesterol, although fats contribute most.

In the 1950s many American scientists decided that it was not just fat that caused cholesterol to increase in the arteries, but a particular kind of fat. Ordinary fat molecules are saturated by hydrogen atoms, but some fats are unsaturated. These "polyunsaturates" have become very popular as a method of reducing cholesterol in the blood.

Cited as proof of the polyunsaturate theory was the fact that the Danes, who eat lots of butter and "hard" cheese, suffer from atherosclerosis, while the Italians, who consume more unsaturates, such as olive oil and "soft" cheese, rarely have the disease. And the Japanese, whose diet contains more fish than any other nation's, also rarely had atherosclerosis until recently, when their diet began to change. Fish, like olive oil, is high in polyunsaturated fats. Despite their modest diet and economic status, the Japanese have long been a healthy nation. However, with increasing affluence and an acquired taste for pleasanter foods, they too are beginning to suffer from heart trouble and other deadly ills that plague the overeating nations of the world.

WHY WE EAT TOO MUCH

Physiologists believe that there is an appetite control or regulator in the brain. Called, appropriately, the "appestat," this center is in the hypothalamus, an organ at the base of the brain. The appestat appears to consist of two distinct parts, a "feeding center" that triggers our desire to eat, and a "satiation center" that turns it off. One theory is that the appestat is controlled by the amount of glucose in the system.

In earlier times it was thought that the sense of hunger was caused by the pangs in the stomach as it contracted. However, this would hardly have worked with primitive man, who may not have known even that his stomach was connected with his mouth. Experiments have shown that even with nerves from the stomach cut, hunger still affects animals in the normal way and causes them to eat. The "hungry pain" in our stomach is merely incidental.

Interestingly, it has been found that in small children, and in all lower animals, specific hunger behavior results in craving and eating the proper foods when they are available. However, this ability seems lost in some adults, and it is believed that learned tastes, habitual overeating, and other such cultural and social influences "mask" the natural ability to satisfy specific hungers. In one experiment the adrenal glands of laboratory animals were severed, a surgery that makes it necessary for the animals to consume far more salt to stay alive. And the animals spontaneously did just this, eating sufficient extra quantities to balance their body chemistry even without the aid of the adrenal glands.

There is some evidence, too, suggesting that our practice of setting regular mealtimes convenient to our work and other habits may contribute to overeating. Man once ate when food was available, or when he got hungry. Now we have become conditioned to "getting hungry at mealtime." Tests made with rats show that those permitted to snack, that is, to eat when they wanted to, did not accumulate as much fat as those fed on a regular schedule of meals. Unfortunately, many humans snack *in addition* to regular meals, and thus make the problem worse!

It seems evident that in some of us the appestat does not function properly, either because of man's decreased physical efforts, or because of modern diet. Experiments with animals show that when the feeding center is removed the animal suffers from a condition called *anorexia,* or lack of appetite. A few humans suffer from this condition, and some deaths result from it. Relatively few of us have this problem, however. Instead, we literally don't seem to know when to quit eating once our appestats have turned us on. Interestingly, experiments with rats show that when the satiation center is damaged the animals eat ravenously, and some gain weight until they are four times or more their normal weight. This extreme

For most of the world, malnutrition is the worst food problem. This little girl is trying valiantly to like the new mix of TMP (texture mung protein) with rice and vegetables produced by the U.N. Food and Agricultural Organization's Freedom from Hunger program in Thailand. High-protein food supplements from local mung and soybean crops protect young children from protein-calorie malnutrition. FAO Photo by F. Botts.

ratio is about the limit for humans too, and sideshows exhibit human overeaters weighing 800 pounds or so.

Pleasure is part of the problem, too. We are far more likely to overeat when the food is pleasant-tasting than we are when it is neutral to the palate or actually bad-tasting. Those concerned with malnutrition in various parts of the world deplore the fact that most peoples take readily to candy and soft drinks but it is difficult to get them to eat highly nutritious protein food supplements because they are not as pleasant to the taste. Even those rats that had become heavyweight, compulsive eaters ate less when their food was dosed with cellulose to make it unappetizing or with quinine to make it taste unpleasant.

EATING LESS FOR HEALTH

In the face of starvation in other countries, the National Academy of Science in the United States in 1964 recommended that the caloric intake for American men be reduced from 3200 daily to 2900. Even this approximately 10 percent reduction leaves us overweight on the average. Tests with rats show that underweight is a better condition than overweight and perhaps even better than average weight! For the thin rats, while maturing more slowly, lived longer. Of course there is more to life than living longer, but for those who think they could make such longevity worth while, a reduction in weight would seem to be a good insurance policy.

There are two ways to lose weight. The first is to burn off the calories with physical work; the second is not to consume the calories in the first place. Unfortunately, most Americans are attempting to use the first approach, which could bring with it other benefits like harder muscles, better physique, and better health and resistance to illness. But it takes more willpower than most of us have to stick to an effective exercise, which may be inconvenient and boring. So we jog a few times, or ride an exercise machine furiously for short periods, and then lamely give it up. For most of us it is going to take the "won't power" of cutting food intake rather than the willpower of exercise.

Encouragingly there are an increasing number of sensible dietary weight-reduction programs now available, and more and more physicians are learning how to treat their obese and overweight patients. The cautious use of drugs can help those with psychological eating problems and even make it easier for those who simply like to eat. However, drugs themselves can cause what may prove to be greater problems, and it is best to do without them if possible.

Crash diets, abstention from drinking water, and sweat baths and other beauty salon treatments for removing weight are bound to be shortlived in effect and futile. It is far better to adopt a sensible diet that will reduce weight *gradually*—say a pound a week or even a pound a month—and then to increase that diet slightly when weight is reduced to the proper level. Ideally, there should be a combination of proper diet and proper exercise, for physical condition is an important factor in being able to assimilate our food properly. Someone with poor circulation and muscle tone has a difficult time properly handling the food intake.

It has been found in work with obese patients that when food is stripped of its attractive appearance, the candlelight and wine, the camaraderie of the coffee break, and so on, actual body needs take over from appetite and the patient eats only what is proper for him. Thus much of the overeating problem may be psychological rather than physiological. Many of us eat for pure pleasure, substituting food for other pleasures we are missing. For most of us, sweets, steaks, rich sauces and gravies, even without psychological problems, are pure pleasure to eat, and we eat them to excess. Not many of us would stuff ourselves on tasteless bread, watery soups, or flavorless meats and vegetables.

WE ARE WHAT WE EAT

A sixteenth-century painter, Giuseppe Arcimboldo, painted an unusual "portrait" of a man literally made of food; a pickle for a nose, peaches for cheeks, a pear for a chin, and so on; with even an "ear" of corn! While such an interpretation is unrealistic, we are to a great extent what we eat: our bodies are built from the proteins, the fats, and the carbohydrates we consume. Vitamins and minerals—including water, incidentally—are also vital intakes.

Not all of us eat the same foods. There are those who for one reason or another shun meats, and some people even refuse to eat meat products such as milk, cheese and eggs. These vegetarians sometimes eat no meat because of religious or moral reasons. Author George Bernard Shaw, for instance,

Sprightly vegetarian George Bernard Shaw takes a walk on his 79th birthday. Shaw died in 1950 at the age of 94. Associated Press Photo.

objected that he was of such a nature as to be unable to eat corpses! His meatless diet, he claimed, made him ten times as healthy as "an ordinary carcass eater"—despite the fact that the "carcass" had consumed ten times as much plant food as Shaw had. Shaw did live to a ripe old age and was an accepted genius, but it is doubtful that either of these accomplishments can be attributed to his all-plant diet.

Mahatma Gandhi was another famous vegetarian. He abstained from animal flesh for religious reasons and also on principle. He tried a diet of meat once but could not tolerate it, yet he was fond of quoting a little jingle on the subject:

> Behold the mighty Englishman —
> He rules the Indian small,
> Because being a meat-eater
> He is five cubits tall.

There is a good bit of poetic exaggeration here, of course, since the average Englishman is nowhere near 7½ feet tall! However, meat eating is associated with physical strength, and there are warrior tribes that eat meat almost exclusively.

Vilhjalmur Stefansson, the Arctic explorer who was also a knowledgeable nutritionist, lived for a year on nothing but fish, animal products, meat, and water in apparent good health for a test. He had previously lived for ten years on Mackenzie Island with Eskimos who ate nothing but meat and fish. And Stefansson too lived a long and active life.

While by careful selection a vegetarian can find all the necessary food constituents, it is a risky diet. Oftentimes those who adopt it by choice or of necessity are short of vitamins, certain amino acids, and so on. It is doubtful, too, that all could do as well on nothing but meat as Stefansson did, although meat does contain all the needed amino acids, as well as carbohydrates and fats. Most nutritionists feel that there should be a balance of carbohydrates, fats and protein, achieved through a diet consisting at least partly of animal protein, or fish at the least. If there is a perfect food it is probably milk, as is obvious from observing babies and animal young who live and grow rapidly on a strict diet of milk. Indeed, it is when the children of certain lands have to shift to other kinds of food that their troubles start.

There are health foods and health fads, including the popular one of eating only "organic foods" rather than those chemically fertilized and protected from pests. There is nothing wrong with such "natural" foods, of course, but neither is there anything wrong, usually, with the chemically fertilized foods that most of us manage to stay alive on. Of course people do die from spoiled and poisoned foods.

Even the health food addict's blackstrap molasses and yogurt are fine, if they are not relied on to provide all necessary nourishment, and if we do not expect from them all the miracles promised by some unscrupulous "experts." Among other touted health foods are wheat germ, brewers' yeast, and soybeans. Soybeans are an excellent food, high in protein. So are lima beans; in fact, they are perhaps the most nutritionally balanced vegetable or legume we can eat, with almost all the necessary constituents.

There are some health food regimens, however, that are dangerous, and it is estimated that each year Americans part with half a billion dollars for phony miracle foods that do not do what they are claimed to do and may even harm the consumer. While food is vitally important, it is not to be credited or blamed for all conditions of health or sickness. We may eat a perfect diet and still come down with a disease; and we may be very healthy without a "perfect" diet. Most of us do not suffer from some sort of nutritional deficiency, unless it be common sense for not eating too much, and only some diseases can be laid at the doorstep of diet.

FOOD—A MATTER OF LIFE OR DEATH

Our ancestors ate both meat and vegetables. So while it is possible to survive on either exclusively, a diet of both is probably to be preferred. All the questions of what things are best to eat, and in what quantities, have not yet been settled. We will probably continue to learn new and valuable lessons in nutrition in the years ahead.

There is nothing we buy that is as important to life as food. Without it we die. But too much or the wrong kind can kill us. We owe it to ourselves, and to coming generations as well, to know enough about food so that we properly nourish ourselves. And we owe it to those who are starving to do all we can to feed them—or better yet, to help them feed themselves.

CHAPTER
2

The Great Food Chain

From ancient times until very recently, men thought plants drew their substance from the soil. When the physician and alchemist Jan Helmont proved through experiments early in the seventeenth century that no weight was taken from the ground by a tree he planted and carefully observed, he declared that all organic matter came from the water the roots drew in. Today we know that while plants contain much water, there is another major component, carbon dioxide, that gives organic matter the property of life.

We make many things from plastics, but we will never be able to make plastic food. Food is different from other substances in that it contains energy. Now, gasoline and wood contain energy and we cannot eat them, so there are further qualities necessary for food. Food must be organic (derived from living things) and in a form our bodies can make use of. Energy, however, is the basis for food, and the original source of that energy is the sun.

The sun supplies most of the energy to drive our engines and motors, and we draw on the sun for this energy in the amount of about 4½ billion horsepower. Coincidentally, at the present time we require just about the same amount of energy in our food—energy that must also come from the sun. There is no danger that we shall run short of solar energy in the near future, for the sun showers the earth with the fantastic total of about 228 *trillion* horsepower in the form of electromagnetic radiation. Only a very tiny part of this radiation is used by plants to accomplish the magic of photosynthesis, the conversion of solar energy into food energy in carbohydrates.

PHOTOSYNTHESIS

Mushrooms grow in the dark by a process not involving photosynthesis, and yeast, too, grows without help from the sun. But the overwhelming bulk of our food depends on the sun for life and growth. The "independent plants," those that grow because of sunlight, are also called green plants. The green color of leaves comes from the chemical chlorophyll contained in the plant's cells. Chlorophyll is a catalyst, or speeder-up of chemical actions, and permits the marvel of plant growth in light.

Each plant cell is a tiny chemical factory. It uses only two chemicals for its basic action: water and carbon dioxide. We are familiar with carbon dioxide in its frozen form (dry ice), since it is often used to keep things cold. It also produces a foam for firefighting. In nature it is an invisible, odorless gas. How can plants grow from just water and such a gas? This is the miracle of plant life, the wonder of chlorophyll-assisted photosynthesis (the synthesis or building up of something with the help of light).

Through its cell walls, a plant takes in carbon dioxide from the air (or from water, as in the case of marine plants) and water, in the form of ocean or lake water, water in the soil, or water vapor. In the chemical factory of the plant leaf, carbon dioxide and hydrogen are mixed in a very special way. Now, water can be broken down into its parts of hydrogen and oxygen by the process of electrolysis. This may be accomplished with electricity, but it can also be done by sunlight under very special conditions. These conditions are present in the green plant, particularly with chlorophyll helping. As a catalyst it makes much more of the light usable in the process.

Water is H_2O. Carbon dioxide is CO_2. When hydrogen is removed from water, oxygen remains. This is given off by the plant, a by-product that is most important and continually purifies the air around plants, fields, and forests. Something even more important happens to the freed hydrogen. It is combined with the carbon dioxide to produce a chemical compound known as CH_2O. And this is a very special compound—an "organic" compound, called a carbohydrate; and a carbohydrate, of course, is food.

Here's what the chemical equation for photosynthesis looks like:

$$H_2O + CO_2 + \frac{\text{light energy}}{112 \text{ kilocalories}} = CH_2O + O_2$$

Here is the source of the kilocalories we count in our daily diet. Since sunlight is the original source of the energy in all organic matter and all life energy on earth, it is literally sunshine that we eat for energy to go about our daily lives.

A most important thing to remember is that while carbon, hydrogen and oxygen are not destroyed but simply changed from one form to another in the endless life cycle on earth, there is one ingredient of food that *is* lost each time we eat. This is the energy portion, the kilocalories we get from the sun. This solar energy must be replenished with each cycle, if life is to go on. The energy in our foods is given back to the environment as heat and to all intents is gone forever, unlike the material components of food.

While carbon, hydrogen, and oxygen are sufficient to make the basic carbohydrate matter in plants, as a practical matter there are other elements that enter the combination. Nitrogen is one of these, and it is nitrogen that is the principle component of what are called proteins. Nitrogen is a fertilizer, as are sulfur, phosphorus, and some other elements. Nature provides these, as is obvious from plants that grow with no help from man. But for our agriculture it is almost always necessary to add nutrients in appreciable quantities. For example, a ton of crops can take almost 100 pounds of fertilizer from the soil.

While man has learned to fix nitrogen from the atmosphere, plants that perform the miracle of photosynthesis cannot match this feat. Nitrogen must be taken in through the plant's roots, usually assisted by certain bacteria that cluster there in a host-parasite relationship with the plant. Since the plants constantly take nitrogen from the soil, man must put it back if he hopes to produce crops regularly.

HOW MUCH FOOD?

Perhaps only about two-tenths of one percent of the total sun energy falling on crops is converted in the process. Nevertheless, on a worldwide basis green plants each year convert about 100 billion tons of elemental carbon from carbon dioxide into organic forms of carbohydrates. This is just the carbon part of organic matter, and when we add the weight of water and oxygen, the total weight of carbohydrates is perhaps 350 billion tons. Of course, not all of this plant life is fit for food. It is estimated that 10^{19} kilocalories of energy are stored in plants each year. This is 10,000,000,000,000,000,000 or 10 million trillion kilocalories, enough for ten trillion people to have a diet of about 2750 calories a day, something over what we now average! However, only a tiny fraction of this energy ever becomes available to us as food.

Each square yard of the earth's surface, in clear air and with the sun shining perpendicularly on it as at high noon, receives about one horsepower of sunshine. One hour of this radiation at midday produces one horsepower-hour of energy. We can translate this into kilocalories to relate it better to food energy. One horsepower-hour is equivalent to about 640 kilocalories; thus five hours of direct sunlight on one square yard is more than equivalent to the average food-energy intake of the best-fed (or most-fed) peoples of the earth!

This does not mean that one person could be sustained by a one-square-yard garden plot, unfortunately. First of all, sunlight does not always strike the ground vertically; most of the time it is at quite an angle, and this reduces the total energy. And for more than half the 24-hour day there is no sunlight at all. Next come the losses in converting solar energy into food energy we can use. Photosynthesis converts only about 1/500th of the energy of the sun that reaches earth into organic matter. For practical reasons man-raised crops are grown on separate plants with some space "wasted" between them, including furrows for watering.

Much laboratory research has been done on the phenomenon of photosynthesis, and some workers claim to have greatly increased the conversion efficiency under such conditions. In fact, one scientist named Otto Warburg has performed experiments that he declared produced perfect, 100 percent conversion of light to food energy. Few others accept this claim any more than they do the notion of a perpetual-motion machine or a machine without friction. It is possible that the photosynthetic process can be improved, of course, particularly since there remains more than 99.8 percent room for such improvement. One possibility is the addition of more carbon dioxide to the air. In nature, there is only a tiny amount of this gas in the atmosphere, and by increasing this to as much as 3 percent the scientists investigating photosynthesis have been able to increase yields of organic matter under laboratory conditions.

We could live on food raised in a "garden" 36 inches on a side if we could perfect the photosynthetic process and prevent clouds from blocking out light from our tiny farm. This is the goal awaiting some future geniuses in the food field. For the present, we are limited by a great number of practical considerations.

The range of production of organic matter per square yard varies from as low as a tenth of a gram per day for barren desert and some parts of the ocean to as high as 25 grams per day in certain efficiently cultivated farmland or in polluted water. The worldwide average production of grain is only about two grams per square yard per day.

Here is the worldwide per capita yearly average for food production:

Grains	660 pounds
Vegetables	300 pounds
Fruits	200 pounds
Milk	250 pounds
Fish	35 pounds
Meat	34 pounds
Totals:	1479 pounds of food per person per year

This amounts to slightly more than four pounds of food daily per person—man, woman, child, and infant—in the world. It represents more than 5,000 calories, far more than even a fat man's diet. An important factor in the great food chain, then, is distribution, and this is part of the problem of hunger and malnutrition in the world today. For the average intake of calories worldwide is less than half of 5,000.

Perhaps 10 percent of the ice-free surface of the earth is now under cultivation, although it is estimated that almost 25 percent is potentially arable, or fit for raising food crops. There are certain limitations, of course, in that many areas do not have sufficient water. In others it is too hot or too cold, and in some the soil is not good enough to support growth or is not even soil but rock.

The oceans are more than twice the total land area, and all of the sea is potentially fit for the growth of marine plants, so some people think that the sea should yield far more of our food than it does at present. For instance, it is pointed out that while land cultivation takes place in relatively thin strips of soil and air, marine life can grow to great depths. And there is 100 times as much carbon in water as there is in the air.

However, there are also many factors that work to reduce the sea's plant potential. First, while there is much carbon, there is little nitrogen, the much-needed fertilizer for plants. Second, there are "marine deserts," just as there are arid deserts on dry land. The water just does not contain sufficient nutrients to produce much plant life. And growth takes place only in the "photic" layer of the sea, extending to about 300 feet deep. This is the distance that sufficient light penetrates to accomplish photosynthesis. For these and perhaps other reasons, the sea does not produce as much life as it might be thought capable of. However, some authorities believe it may produce as much as 90 percent of the plant life on earth.

Another reason why all the potential food energy produced by plants is not available to man is that we rely on plants for many things besides food. Wood, for example, represents a great part of the plant output. Even with plastic and other products supplanting wood in many uses, cellulose, wood fiber, is the basis for many of the new products used in building and elsewhere.

We grow flowers and lawns just for enjoyment where in olden times family goats and cows and other animals once munched the grass in the yard, performing duty as gardeners and also producing meat and milk from plants that otherwise would be wasted. We keep pets, too, supporting a large "biomass," or weight of living animals, unproductive for food and using food. One authority has estimated that a third of the canned fish in the United States is fed to pet cats. Another says that a fair-sized country could be fed with the food we buy for our pets. It is pointed out that "there are no dogs in China." If we can control our population growth we may be able to continue to feed ourselves and our pets and to raise our lawns, flowers, and parks. Food for the soul is almost as important as wheat and meat.

ECOLOGY

Benjamin Franklin once remarked that if there were but one species of life it would eventually blanket the earth. Fortunately there are countless species of both plants and animals, each in relatively small numbers, sharing the blessings of the land and the oceans. There are no "monopolies" in nature, although at times some individual populations do seem to run wild for a brief period before various checks and balances reduce them to normal numbers or less.

The food chain is part of a larger overall natural system called ecology, which means the relationships between living creatures and their environment. There are a number of ecologic interactions that have a bearing on man and food, including "commensalism," "symbiosis," "competition," "predation," and "parasitism."

Commensalism translates literally into "sitting down at the same table." There are commensal rats, so called because they derive their food from man's supply and eat it in his environment. There are also small fish that sneak into sea anemones and eat pieces of other fish the anemones have captured. A tragic form of commensalism occurs when starving human beings are reduced to seeking scraps of food in garbage.

Symbiosis, sometimes called mutualism when the interaction is beneficial to both parties, includes the relationships of small shrimp and the large fish whose teeth they clean in exchange for the scraps of food they find in the mouth of the host. There is also mutualism in the case of man and the bacteria that reside in his intestines performing a valuable service in exchange for food. These microorganisms help us to digest and synthesize some vitamins we need.

Competition is simply the battle of two or more species for the same food supply. Grasshoppers and locusts eat up man's crops, and men and bears compete with bees for the honey they produce.

Predation is the killing and eating of one species by another. Cows eat clover or hay: men eat cows. Cats kill mice, which feed on small animals. On rare occasions animals eat men, and sometimes an animal eats another of the same species. This of course is cannibalism, a form of predation from which even man is not free.

Parasitism technically is the living of a very small species on another species. Dogs have ticks; sometimes men have ringworm or other parasite infestations. Sometimes that term is extended to include all those who live on other forms of life; in which case it includes everything but the plants, which derive their energy from the sunshine. Man plays host to countless parasites. Some unfortunate people at times are infested with tiny insects. All of us play host to millions of far tinier parasites in the form of bacteria. Man himself is a parasite in the sense that he lives on other animals or on plants. We must feed ourselves indirectly by preying on plants or plant-eating animals. This is the "great food chain" so important to us.

THE PYRAMID OF FOOD

Sometimes the food chain is described more accurately as a "pyramid." At its broad base are the green plants. Next higher are the herbivores, or plant-eaters. Then come the predators, which prey on the smaller animals. There may be several levels of these meat-eating carnivores. Finally, at the top of the pyramid, stands man himself. Yet, ironically, man is host to all the tiny parasites we have mentioned. Actually the food chain, or pyramid, is not a neat and easily diagrammed process. Even the word "web," which is sometimes used to describe it, does not do justice to its complexities.

One thing making the food chain far more complicated than a simple diagram might make it appear is the place of insects in the total scheme of things. Generally we do not eat insects, although it is possible to purchase chocolate-covered ants and grasshoppers in some specialty stores. There are primitive tribes who do regularly eat insects, however, and the Bible tells of John the Baptist living on locusts and honey—honey itself being produced by other insects. There are about 10,000 species of insects that prey on man's food. Many insects also help, like the bee already mentioned. Other insects pollinate plants and thus make it possible for us to cultivate those crops. Some insects control others that are pests. It would be impossible, or at least very unwise, to wipe out all insects. But some species do not seem to have a place of value in the ecological system, and man has eradicated and will continue to eradicate some species, like the tsetse fly, screwworm fly, bollworm, melon fly, and mosquito.

Other parasites can also play havoc with crops. Rabbits are among these, as are rats. Birds do millions of dollars worth of damage to our crops in the United States alone. Yet sometimes man in his attempts to improve the food chain has caused irreparable harm instead.

The Great Food Chain • 23

While the plants make it possible for animals to live, animals too perform services that keep plants living and producing. This intermeshed life cycle has evolved over millions of years and, while seemingly simple, is most complex and delicately balanced. When we breathe, we take in oxygen to "burn" up our foodstuffs and produce energy. We breathe out carbon dioxide, the vital raw material in plant production of carbohydrates by photosynthesis. All animals produce carbon dioxide, as do plants themselves in rotting vegetation. The decaying plant matter also provides needed nutrients for new plants. So do dead animal matter and animal waste products. The same atoms of carbon, hydrogen, and oxygen have recycled through the ages, with nothing lost or gained in the total system. Only the incoming solar energy is new, and this must be constantly replaced as our earth turns to face the sun each day.

From the human standpoint, the ideal food situation would be a chain in which there were only primary producers of food (the plants), meat animals, and man, the consumer. In actuality, there are many nonproducers in the chain. An example of this on a simplified scale is a newly opened fishing pond. It is stocked with marine plants on which small fish feed, and these in turn feed larger fish, which fishermen catch for food. The system is relatively efficient, with little food wasted in the chain. But as time goes on, more and more herbivores are added to the pond—small fish not suitable for larger fish to eat, bottom creatures the fish can't catch, and insects that eat plants but contribute nothing. So the yield of food fish for man shrinks because more and more of the constant primary plant production is eaten by outsiders and wasted, as far as human food is concerned.

Thus it is sometimes desirable to drain the pond and start all over again with only the necessary links in the chain. While this is simple in a small pond, it is difficult with a lake or large reservoir. Extending the problem to the entire world, we are simply stuck with the situation and cannot "start over" again!

This may actually be a blessing in disguise, for some ecologists believe that a great variety of species in an environment make that environment more stable. For example, suppose man depended entirely on wheat for food and there were hundreds of millions of acres planted to wheat and nothing else—no animals, insects, or anything but wheat—except, that is, a virus blight that one day wiped out the wheat. Man too would be wiped out, unless he could feed on the virus, which is unlikely. However if, in addition to the wheat, there were rice, corn, barley, oats, vegetables, fruits, and many animals, the loss of wheat, although catastrophic, would not mean the end of humankind. As best he could, man would switch to other foods. Perhaps some little-known species of plant might save the day.

Here is an example of changing environment and the supplanting of one food species by another: Some years ago commercial duck raising became popular on Long Island, and roast Long Island duckling in orange sauce became a favorite dish. The ducks, however, contributed large amounts of organic manure to the waters of the Sound, and the dominant plankton could not tolerate this sudden overfertilization. However, a rare species was able to turn the fertilizer to growth, and it became dominant and actually increased the marine life in the Sound. However, the oysters formerly commercially raised could not use the new plankton for food and died out. Without the rare species waiting to take over, conditions would of course have been even worse, and *no* appreciable marine life could have been supported.

THE ENVIRONMENT'S "LAW OF TITHES"

One basic fact of food life is that the biomass of each higher level of the living pyramid or chain decreases. Plants, at the bottom, represent the greatest weight. Because no conversion process is perfectly efficient, the herbivores who feed on plants must weigh much less than the plants. And man must be less in weight on a biomass basis than the levels below him. In fact, one authority has estimated that the food animals man depends on represent a population of 15 billion equivalents coexisting on earth with us!

Just as a plant cannot convert all the solar energy striking it into food energy, neither can a cow browsing on vegetation turn all of that into meat or milk. There is an ecological "law of tithes" because of this, saying that each higher level on the food pyramid produces only one pound of weight for ten pounds of food eaten. This is of course a very inexact rule of thumb, since some consumers are not even ten-percent efficient, and some, like poultry and hogs fattened under carefully controlled conditions, may return as much as a pound of meat for each two pounds of food.

Ten acres of grain might feed ten people. But the beef cattle raised on ten acres of grain will feed only one. At first glance this highly inefficient conversion of plants to meat seems to suggest that we should stop eating meat and become plant-eating vegetarians. The same situation, on an even more lopsided scale, prevails in the oceans of the world. Our fishermen's catch represents hundreds or thousands of pounds of plankton for each pound of food fish. It would seem logical to eat the plankton instead, and there are indeed some who advocate this approach and try to design schemes for doing it. However, there are good reasons why man eats meat and fish, rather than adopting vegetarianism as some groups do.

To begin with, not all cattle are fed grain that man could have made into bread or other food. Many, in fact, subsist entirely on forage that man cannot use for food at all. Even in the United States, where our tastes in meat dictate feeding cattle some grain, from 60 percent to 90 percent of their diet comes from grass or other rangeland vegetation on which man would starve to death. And some cattle are fed on such substances as urea and cellulose, more animal food useless to man.

It is also true that goodly amounts of grain are used in America and elsewhere in well-to-do countries as cattle food. While this practice might be attacked on strictly nutritional grounds, economically it can be defended. In the United States, even with less land in use now than in the past, there have been large surpluses of grain since the developing countries have been able to produce nearly all their own needs. Thus the farmer has a choice of using grain as cattle feed or not being able to use it at all.

Finally, meat is the best source of protein of all the foods, and practically all authorities agree that the world should eat more and and not less meat. While it would be good if the fishmeal produced from much of the ocean catch could nourish humans directly, it seems impossible to get many people to eat it. They will eat poultry and hogs fed on it, however. And the conversion from feed to human food in this case is fairly efficient.

In the sea there are even more links to the food chain, more levels to the food pyramid. The green plants are the *phytoplankton,* or floating plant plankton, that turn solar energy into carbohydrates. Feeding on these are the still tiny *zooplankton,* or animal plankton. Small fish feed on these and are in turn eaten by larger fish. Again, man is the ultimate consumer atop the marine food pyramid. Seaweed is used more than any other form of marine plant, being used as feed for sheep in the Orkney Islands and eaten by some peoples. However, seaweeds represent less than one percent of marine plant growth and are not an especially attractive food source to begin with.

26 • FEAST AND FAMINE

The German chemist Fritz Haber gave the world the principle of the "fixation" of nitrogen from the air and thus assured a good supply of fertilizer for our crops. Haber also tried to find a way to strain out the gold in the sea, for it is there in billion-dollar quantities. Unfortunately for him, and for Germany's post World War I economy, Haber's process was too costly for the tiny amounts of the precious metal it was able to extract. The same general principle prevents us from making use of minute plankton cells as food. Millions of gallons of sea water would have to be strained to

Lower left: A plankton sampler aboard the research vessel *Siscowet* on Lake Superior.

Plankton comprise the bottom step of the great food pyramid. This single diatom (lower right) represents a species common in the Great Lakes and also important in the diet of larval sea lampreys. Bureau of Commercial Fisheries Photos.

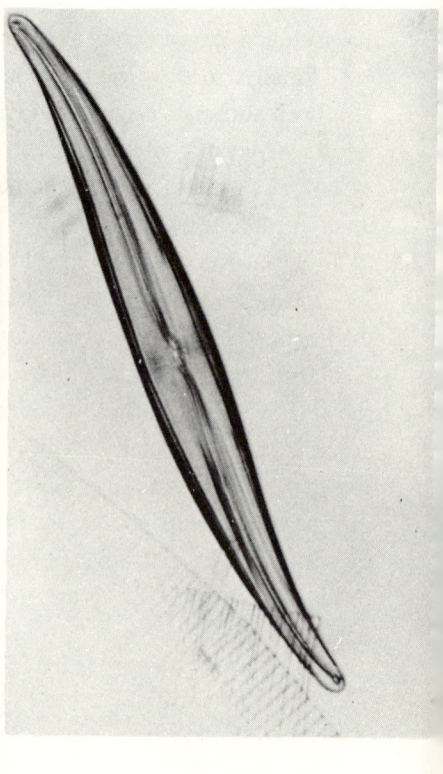

produce a single pound of plankton. And unlike gold, plankton is not a very valuable commodity. Food is an economic proposition as well as one of nutrition, and the plankton strainers are doomed by high costs and low market prices. Some fish catches bring only a few cents a pound, and fish is a more desirable food than plankton would be.

Many nutritionists feel that there is a great misuse in the ocean's produce, however, in the conversion of a large percentage of the catch to animal feed. Until Peru entered the fishing world a relatively short time ago, 95 percent of the catch was being made in the Northern Hemisphere. Now the southern waters provide about 35 percent of the total. Yet practically all the billions of pounds of anchovies caught by Peruvians are sold as fish meal to feed chickens and hogs in America, Japan, and Western Europe.

WILD ANIMALS FOR FOOD

Because man was once primarily a hunter of wild animals for food, it is natural that many of us still have the desire to hunt and fish and still pursue these hobbies quite vigorously. In fact, sportfishing in the United States alone is a $2 billion-a-year business, far exceeding the value of the fish brought home from lake, stream, or ocean. However, there are several pounds of fish, on the average, caught by sport fisherman for each of us a year. Hunters bring home everything from game birds and rabbits to deer, wild pigs, and bear. In some communities these are an important source of food on the table. The advantage of catching wild animals is that they seldom compete for food with man or meat animals, require no expense for raising, and are generally immune to diseases that may plague domestic animals.

It should be obvious that man is chained to nature for his food supply. We have the tendency to forget that milk is not produced in a factory, and that our foods are not manufactured as our automobiles and television sets are. The truth is that we sit atop a food pyramid dependent on the sun, the green plants, and several levels of intermediate life forms. Only when all these levels function, only when the chain is unbroken, is man secure at the top of the food heap.

It follows, then, that we must be aware of the vital steps in the production of our food, the many complex factors of physical laws that are involved—solar radiation, water, weather, fertilization, animals, insects, and disease—as well as of the processes harvesting, processing, preservation, and distribution that man himself can control to some degree. There are many links in our food chain, and like most chains it is no stronger than the weakest link. Let's make sure man is not that weakest link!

CHAPTER
3

Converting Food and Energy

A green plant puts energy from the sun into its cells as carbohydrates. We eat those carbohydrates and reverse the process, taking that energy *out* of the foodstuffs. Although most of us take this process for granted—and man and lower animals have been doing this for ages—the extraction of energy from organic material is just as much a miracle as that performed by the plant and its chlorophyll.

The ancient Greeks were perhaps the first to investigate why we ate food and what became of it. When men had time to think, instead of spending all their days seeking food to keep them alive, they began to study the body and its functions. Food intake was obviously such an important part of the process of living that ancient medical men linked it with disease. We know today that food is indeed responsible for many ills and also for many cures.

As early as Hippocrates, men theorized that food was "cooked" inside the body to provide energy needed for living. They knew that air was part of the cooking process, and that cooking, which required fire, could not proceed without air. They knew this in a vague and general way, of course, with many errors in their attempts to make specific diagrams of what happened. Just as man did not understand the circulation of blood until long after he knew its purpose, early nutritionists also missed the mark. However, Erasistratus, who was born in 304 B.C., noticed in animal experiments that the weight of body wastes was far less than the weight of food and drink consumed. As he put it, ". . . there has been a great loss of weight, plainly because, perceptible only to the reason, a copious emanation has taken place."

This emanation was part of the metabolism, the process of living. Body heat and perspiration were given off all the time, and unless food was consumed to replace that heat the body would consume its own substance until starvation resulted.

The concept of the body as a sort of living furnace, burning fuel with great drafts of air just as a blacksmith's forge requires air to burn coal, is many centuries old. But for many centuries the idea did not progress beyond that general concept. Not until 1614 did a scientist named Sanctorius extend Erasistratus's reasoning and substitute himself for the bird Erasistratus put in a pot and weighed from day to day. He reported that "if eight pounds of meat and drink are taken in one day, the quantity that usually goes off by insensible perspiration in that time is five pounds." That much fuel was burned, leaving less weight in ash or waste products.

Jan B. van Helmont, the Belgian physician who was interested in digestion among many other things, was born in 1577. About the time Sanctorius was weighing himself and his food intake, Helmont thought he had proved that a tree grew not because of the earth it rooted in but because of the water that irrigated it. He was partially correct, of course, but he did not include carbon dioxide as the other component of the tree's organic matter. Helmont coined the name "gas" for the vapors he studied, naming them *chaos* because they were in such a state of turmoil, but spelling the word phonetically so that it came out "gas." And Helmont also isolated carbon dioxide, the gas that combines with water to produce organic matter! Helmont called it "gas sylvestre," or wood gas, because he produced it by burning wood.

In 1774 the English chemist Joseph Priestley discovered oxygen, although he called it "dephlogisticated air." The scientific stage was then set for the final work of establishing what really took place in the human furnace. French scientist Antoine Lavoisier has been called the father of chemistry, and among his contributions to knowledge was the demonstration that fire is the "oxidation" of fuel. He also established the fact that

"Life is a chemical function," Lavoisier's studies revealed. His theory was the basis of the science of nutrition. Kean Archives Photo, Phila.

the body's use of food was truly oxidation, a "burning" process, as the ancient Greeks had written. In a series of experiments with animals and later with humans, Lavoisier, assisted by Simon LaPlace, a famous mathematician and astronomer, proved that a guinea pig produced body heat by burning oxygen and food. They observed that the animal also exhaled great quantities of carbon dioxide, the "wood gas" of Helmont.

In 1783 Lavoisier published a paper stating that respiration was actually combustion ". . . admittedly very slow, but otherwise exactly similar to that of charcoal." He burned charcoal to prove that it produced just as much heat from a quantity of oxygen as the guinea pig did.

> Respiration is only a slow combustion of carbon and hydrogen which is entirely similar to that which obtains in a lamp or lighted candle and from this point of view, animals which respire are truly combustible bodies which run and consume themselves. In respiration as in combustion it is the air which furnishes the oxygen . . . but in respiration it is the substance which furnishes the heat . . . if animals do not repair constantly the losses of respiration, the lamp soon lacks oil, and the animal dies, as a lamp goes out when it lacks food.

At last the glimmering seen by early scientists was put down in clear words and numbers: A plant combines water and carbon dioxide with solar energy to produce organic matter. Humans—or lower animals—eat this organic matter as food and then burn it as fuel with oxygen, producing carbon dioxide, water—and energy.

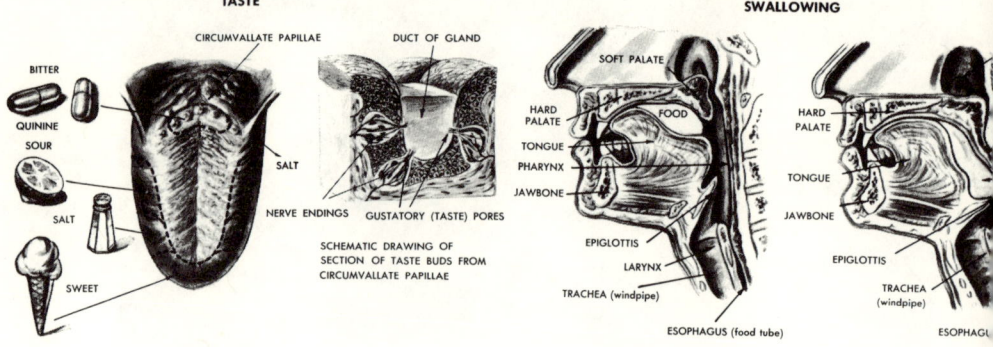

The tongue, along with our olfactory receptors, provides the "proof of the pudding." After that, swallowing—the process diagramed below— is the last voluntary digestive service we provide for our bodies. (Drawings courtesy of the American Medical Association, from *The Wonderful Human Machine*.)

"La vie est un fonction chimique," Lavoisier wrote triumphantly. Life is a chemical function. While this does not begin to say all there is to be said about human life, it formed the basis for the science of nutrition that began to develop soon after Lavoisier was guillotined in the French Revolution on false charges trumped up by his enemies. In the two centuries that have passed since his pioneering guinea-pig-in-the-ice-chamber tests, we have learned much about how the body extracts from foods the energy that bound them together in the first place.

THE DIGESTION OF FOOD

Our mouths water for good food, sometimes just at the sight or even the thought of it, particularly if we are already hungry at the time. Not surprisingly, then, we begin to digest (from a word meaning dissolve) food right in our mouths. Saliva initiates the chemical process of breaking down our food as we chew it. Although saliva is more important as a lubricating medium for the food, there is a "salivary amylase" or enzyme called *ptyalin* present. From a pint to a quart of saliva per day is produced in our mouths. Saliva thoroughly wets the food for later enzyme action in the stomach and elsewhere. It clears the mouth of food particles, softens the food, and helps move it along the alimentary canal.

The teeth serve to grind, cut, and chop our food, thus exposing more of its surface for digestion. The tongue and cheeks help by moving the food around. We only appreciate how complicated a task we do so automatically when something gets out of synchronization and we bite our tongues by mistake! The tongue is also well endowed with taste buds that tell us if food is sweet or sour, salty or bitter. It also can warn us when food is spoiled, although the nose will probably have already told us if this is the case.

Chewed-up food begins its long journey down the alimentary canal, passing first through the pharynx, a tube about five inches long leading to the esophagus. This "gullet" is about twelve inches long and up to an inch in diameter. The swallowing of food, scientifically known as *deglutition,* is a far more complex physical process than we realize as we automatically go about the task. The tongue pushes a ball, or *bolus,* of chewed-up food back to the pharynx. Beyond this, the action of swallowing is not voluntary but automatic on the part of the various concerned parts. The alimentary canal is not the only opening into the mouth, of course. The trachea, or windpipe, is there too, and so are the eustachian tubes connecting the middle ear and the pharynx as well as the nasal passages. To prevent food from entering these (as it sometimes does accidentally, to our great distress), various safeguards operate. While the tongue keeps the food from reentering the mouth, the "soft palate" rises and seals the nasal passages. Muscles close the orifices of the eustachian tubes, and the larynx and epiglottis close off the trachea. "Getting something down the windpipe" is a serious and painful accident that nature carefully guards against.

If you are an informal eater you know that eating can be done while lying down, or even while hanging upside down from a tree branch. This is so because of muscular action, called *peristalsis,* in the esophagus. Surprisingly, not just solid food but liquids too can be consumed in this position. A series of muscles ringing the esophagus alternately contract and expand in a fashion the mechanical engineer wishes he could copy. In this manner, the food is squeezed progressively down (or up, or along!) the esophagus until it reaches the stomach. Not all animals make use of peristalsis, as is evident when chickens pause in their pecking at food to tilt their heads back so gravity can carry grain down their gullets.

THE STOMACH

Although our hearts may be in the right place, the stomach is not where we usually think it is. Actually it is not far below the heart. It is seldom our stomachs that we pat when congratulating ourselves on a good meal. The adult stomach can hold up to three pints, although it frequently seems that we consume much more. The stomach is vaguely described as "bag-shaped" by some writers, and in man there is only one bag. The ruminants, the cud-chewers, including cattle, have several stomachs, which makes it possible for them to digest food we humans cannot handle. Man's stomach is made up of a *corpus,* or forward portion, and an *antrum,* or smaller rearward portion. The entire stomach wall secretes mucus, which protects the delicate lining of the stomach and also moistens the food.

Thus far the bolus, or mouthful, has been treated simply as a glob of food, but in the stomach specialized treatment begins. The main function of this organ is to begin the digestion of protein. Note that we say "begin," for the stomach does only a partial job on this component of our food. Even this, however, calls for some powerful chemical treatment. Some 35 million glands in the stomach release hydrochloric acid and "pepsinogen."

Hydrochloric acid in the stomach also serves to destroy disease bacteria and putrefying bacteria in food. This does not mean that the stomach expects us to be eating spoiled food, although it does happen occasionally and must have happened fairly regularly in primitive times when man did not have food-keeping methods used today. All food contains bacteria, and in time—and at elevated temperatures such as are found in the stomach—these microorganisms grow rapidly. Since food may remain in the stomach for several hours, it has ample time to spoil. This would cause chaos except for the bacteria-killing acid injected from the stomach walls. Were it not for the stomach's mucus lining, the hydrochloric acid that breaks down protein would eat holes in them as well. It does, in fact, when something goes wrong with our digestion. We call the unhappy result stomach ulcers. Mucus also lines the throat and esophagus—and in fact the entire alimentary canal—as protection against sharp particles of food and other potential harm. "Heartburn" occurs when gas from the stomach carries some acid up into the esophagus. Its lining is not sufficiently antacid to make it invulnerable, and we feel a momentary stinging sensation, which has nothing to do with our heart.

Incidentally—or it may have significance nutritionally—the belief that some foods don't stay with us while others "stick to the ribs" is not just imagination. Since carbohydrates are easily digestible, they move through the stomach rapidly. When we eat Chinese food, which is mostly carbohydrates, it really does not stay with us, and although full when we get up from the table, we may be hungry again very soon. Meats and other high-protein foods, on the other hand, take much longer to go through the stomach's digesting process and do "stick to our ribs."

The digestion of carbohydrates by the stomach is negligible, then, although some sucrose may be broken down by the hydrochloric acid. We all have "acid stomachs," and the condition is not something to be worried over and dosed with alkaline preparations. Acid is required to digest our food.

A small amount of fat is digested in the stomach by *lipase,* another enzyme, which can break down finely divided fat, such as that in egg yolk. Another enzyme called rennin precipitates casein from milk; this enzyme is found in very high concentration in infants' stomachs. The rest of us have to depend more on pepsin and acid, for we don't consume as much milk as babies do. Only small amounts of water, salts, alcohol, and glucose are absorbed by the stomach; instead, these pass on to the intestines.

All this time the stomach is not simply lying there and letting the acids and enzymes do all the work. Digestion is not only a chemical process but a physical one as well. Powerful muscles continually contract the stomach walls, making it a kind of churn, a flexible mixing vat that is both container and stirring stick.

The peristaltic contractions in the stomach take place at quite regular rates, varying to as fast as every five seconds. All this kneading and churning action greatly agitates the "chyme," as partially digested food is called.

In ruminants, the antrum portion of the stomach is greatly enlarged to form a "fermentation vat," in which bacteria break down cellulose. Actually, this vat is in two sections, the *rumen* and *reticulum,* which in cows may hold as much as eighty quarts of food! Behind their two forward sections are the *omasum* and the *abomasum.* This last section is generally similar to our stomachs and is the only ruminant stomach containing digestive glands. Cattlemen generally call the first three stomachs of cows the "paunch," the "honeycomb" and the "manyplies," for the second does have a honeycombed lining, and the third has many leaflike folds that practically fill the cavity.

THE INTESTINES

Beyond the stomach, the next portion of the alimentary canal is the small intestine. The "small" refers only to the diameter, from 1½ to 2 inches, since the small intestine is about 22 feet long and coiled many times to fit into the body cavity. In three sections, called the *duodenum*, *jejunum*, and *ileum*, it makes up most of the 30 feet or so of alimentary canal.

When the stomach has finished its chores, it delivers the partially digested food to the small intestine "in spurts." By that time, the salivary amylase has converted as much as 70 percent of the starch or carbohydrates to *maltose*, and many proteins have been broken down to *proteoses* and *peptones*. Only the fat remains largely undigested. The acid balance of the food mass is now between 1.5 and 2.0 pH. But in the duodenum, alkaline secretions change this to a neutral solution. A number of glands in the intestine secrete chemicals to do this job, and so does the pancreas, an organ or gland attached to the intestine. The liver takes part in the chemical process now, too, sending along its bile. Acid neutralization takes place at a certain limited rate, and this is one of the reasons why food comes from the stomach in small amounts at a time. As a matter of fact, it is the acid food itself that regulates its movement. As soon as enough of it has been admitted to acidify the intestine, the stomach closes off.

Properly neutralized, the food moves on through the intestine in its watery bath of juices. It now begins to be broken down finely enough to allow it to be taken into the lining of the intestine, where it will enter the blood or the lymph as nutrients.

The pancreas, a carrot-shaped organ weighing about three ounces, produces the enzyme *trypsin* as its main digestive agent. Trypsin further breaks down the proteins into *polypeptides* and amino acids. A pancreatic amylase called *amylopsin* splits maltose into glucose. A pancreatic *lipase*, called *steapsin*, digests fats, aided by bile salts from the liver. The fat itself helps, forming salts and "soaps" that speed the emulsifying action of the bile salts. Bile is an orange-colored fluid when it comes from the liver, but after storage in the gallbladder it takes on the dark-green, "bilious" color with which we may be familiar. Cholesterol is a component of bile.

Food normally takes about 3½ hours to traverse the many feet of small intestine, being moved along and churned about by peristalic action like that in the esophagus. It is this movement that sometimes becomes audible and embarrassing as a "growling stomach." The absorption of most nutrients from digested food takes place in the small intestine. Proteins are generally absorbed as amino acids, and any whole proteins that do manage to pass through the intestinal walls are in such small amounts as to be of no nutritional significance.

Fatty acids are absorbed from the fat portion of our food intake. Unlike the amino acids, nearly all fat is absorbed into the "lymphatic" system rather than into the blood stream directly. Thus instead of going through the liver with the arterial blood, the fat reaches it through the thoracic lymph duct and the veins. The lymphatic system is a network of fine capillaries similar to those of the bloodstream and lying near the blood capillaries. Lymph, a colorless fluid, is similar to blood except that it has no red corpuscles. The lymphatic system works with the blood to deliver nutrients to body cells and to collect impurities.

Like the amino acids, carbohydrates, in the form of *monosaccharides*, or simple sugars, are absorbed through the intestinal walls and into the bloodstream. Water and undigested food pass on from the small intestine into the large intestine, or colon. The colon is much shorter than the small intestine, and much thicker, being about 2½ inches in diameter. It too is in three portions anatomically, an "ascending colon," or vertically rising section; a "transverse colon," going horizontally across to the other side of the body cavity; and the "descending colon," which drops back down and eventually conducts wastes out of the body.

The undigested food is mainly vegetable matter, and the digestive process continues in the colon. The colon is rich with bacteria which attack the protein and carbohydrates remaining to produce compounds and gases, some of which are absorbed through the walls of the colon. Another important function played by these intestinal bacteria (which of course are parasites that have the cooperative working arrangement known as *symbiosis* with their host, man) is the synthesis of the B vitamins and other vitamins. As in the small intestine, food continues be squeezed and churned as it moves through the colon. Nutrients and water too are absorbed from the material.

DELIVERING FOOD TO THE CELLS

Although after we have eaten a big meal it certainly feels as if we have food inside us, technically speaking food moves through the alimentary canal without really entering the body. In the small intestine, however, about 95 percent of the nutrients do move into the body proper, the other 5 percent being absorbed through the colon. At this point the food has passed from the *chyme,* or partially digested stage, and become *chyle,* a soluble substance ready to be absorbed into the blood.

Just as wonderfully designed as our lungs are to provide more area for the exchange of gases, the intestines are folded, or "convoluted," to provide about three times as much exchange surface as a straight tube would. Additionally, the inner lining of the intestines is covered with millions of fine, almost hairlike projections called *villi.* The Latin word *villus* means shaggy hair. Combined with the already folded surface, the villi give an exchange surface about ten times that of a smooth, unconvoluted shape. In all, the intestines have a total surface area of about 100 feet, five times that of our skin! The villi help stir the chyle as they take in nutrients in the form of amino acids, fatty acids, sugars, vitamins and minerals.

The villi are very small to begin with, but each one is in turn made up of much smaller living cells, and the outer, or *epithelial,* cells are covered with even tinier *microvilli.* There are billions of these compared with the few million villi. And it is through the epithelial cells that absorption takes place. The actual movement of nutrients across the cell-membrane barrier is a chemical and physical miracle using the process of osmosis or liquid pressure and a less-understood mechanism called "active ion transport." Active transport is a process that seems to violate the rules of physics, since the movement is against the pressures that make osmosis possible. Microscopic chemical pumps carry some components in one direction through the cell wall while carrying others in the opposite direction, maintaining a delicate balance all the time.

If all this sounds like hard work for the cells, it is. So hard, in fact, that the epithelial cells have a lifetime of only about two days. At the end of that time they are worn out and must be discarded—as we discard old skin or fingernail filings—and new cells take their places. About half a pound of epithelial cells are consumed every day!

Fat has to be converted to fatty acids to get through the fine filter of the cell wall. But once through, the acids quickly form again into droplets of fat, which are conveyed to the lymph glands.

On their way to the body cells, the nutrients in the blood first reach the liver, a large organ just above the stomach. The liver has been called the most complicated organ in the body. Its spongelike tissues make many needed chemicals in addition to bile; filter out waste products, including ammonia, from the blood; and store up surplus nutrients for later use. Proteins and sugar are stored there, and 95 percent of the body's vitamin A. Only after all this further processing and separating out does the blood then take the nutrients remaining in it to the heart, which pumps them all through the body. The fat, as we mentioned, does not make the trip through the liver but joins the bloodstream farther on.

Even then the nutrient-laden blood is not ready for nourishing the many cells in the body. It must first go to the lungs and pick up the oxidizing agent needed to "burn" the food "fuel." This is oxygen, of course, absorbed from the air we breathe by the *alveoli* of the lungs. Now, with its full component of nutrients and oxygen, the blood begins to distribute them to the trillions of cells throughout the body.

Doing this requires a fantastic plumbing system that engineers can only look at in awe and envy. The aorta, or main artery from the heart, divides into two, and each artery then divides and redivides until there are an estimated sixty miles of *capillaries,* fine bloodcarrying branches only one-fifth the diameter of a human hair. The walls of these capillary tubes are the thickness of one cell, about 1/25,000 of an inch, and molecules of food move easily through them into the hungry cells. While it took the intestines many hours to extract the nutrients from our food, the blood circulation system gets practically all of them to every part of the body in just a few minutes.

There are trillions of cells, and all must be fed. Some of the 45 or 50 nutrients go only to certain cells, such as iodine for the cells of the thyroid gland. Once in the cells, the food does all the varied chores we know it must do; provides heat to keep our temperature near the proper 98.6° F; makes cells grow, and maintains those already fully grown; and powers our muscles so that we can walk and talk, run, smile, think, dream, breathe, and eat to start the nutrition cycle all over again! Carbohydrates are burned for energy and heat. Fats may be similarly handled or stored for future and possible emergency use. Protein, in the form of amino acids, is used in building new tissue for growth and keeping the body's chemistry and machinery going.

MUSCLE-POWER FOR THE HUMAN MACHINE

The conversion of food energy into muscle movement is a fascinating physicochemical process that is a miracle in its own right. The muscles that make it possible to do so many things are marvels of power and efficiency. They are engines with no wheels, gears, or pistons, yet they can still lift a thousand times their weight and, moreover, do it several hundred times a second. And they convert food energy into power with an efficiency that may be as high as 45 percent, compared with only about 10 percent for our automobile engines and a maximum of about 38 percent for our best steam-electric powerplants. Furthermore, muscle is long-lived and self-repairing.

Muscle is protein, built from the amino acids in our food. It consists of tiny rods of *myosin* and *actin,* running lengthwise and overlapping one another. One of the nutrients carried to muscle cells is *adenosine triphosphate,* or ATP, an energy-rich compound. When the proper signal reaches a muscle, myosin enzymes cause stored ATP to give up its energy in a reaction that causes the myosin and actin rods to overlap even more. This thickens the muscle and shortens it, like a rubber band returning to its normal shape after having been stretched.

The simple, one-moving-part muscle engine is not a "heat engine," as are most of man's engines, and it can therefore be more efficient. This efficiency depends on a difference in chemical potential existing in the muscle before and after contraction. The greater the difference, the more efficient the muscle engine. A crude artificial muscle has been put together in the laboratory and made to contract and expand when exposed to different chemical stimuli.

While it is roughly correct to say that man's internal muscle engines operate somewhat like his internal combustion engines in that they burn fuel with air, the analogy is not entirely correct. In subtle ways the human machine is far superior to any man-made machine. Muscle, for example, while powered by food and oxygen, does not have to do its work indirectly, as man does with a steam engine or gasoline engine. In our artificial engines we must produce heat and then use that heat to drive the mechanism, such as a piston. Muscle converts food energy directly into motion, without the intermediate step of producing heat, although some incidental heat is produced by friction within the muscle.

NATURE'S CHEMICAL FACTORY

In green plants, photosynthesis brings water and carbon dioxide together and produces a simple sugar called glucose, the carbohydrate or organic matter we use as food. From that point the plant cell links the simple sugars together as starches, and sometimes even to fats. In a human cell the nutrients go through the reverse process and ultimately are oxidized with oxygen. Water is produced, and so is carbon dioxide. Now we are back where it all began, and as the blood cells deliver oxygen and nutrients into the body cells, they remove carbon dioxide and water from the cells, to be eliminated from the body as waste.

We have noted that the body's enzymes break down protein far more quickly than can the human chemist. But in the cell's metabolism enzymes are capable of extreme slowness when necessary, too. The energy is released at just the right rate for a special reason: An enzyme in body cells converting food to energy as rapidly as pepsin breaks down protein could turn a high-protein meal into sufficient heat to raise the body temperature to 170 degrees, a fever no one could stand!

There are more than 20,000 enzymes manufactured in the body for use in the many and varied chemical processes that must take place in the process we call living. About 1,000 of these have been identified. Their effectiveness is almost unbelievable to those of us who take the process of digestion for granted. It is possible, for example, to break proteins down into their amino-acid components in the laboratory; biochemists do it now to produce artificial or synthetic aminos. It requires boiling at 330° F for about a day in a strong solution of hydrochloric acid. But in the small intestine the process takes place in only a few hours, and in a neutral medium, as we have seen.

It is indeed fortunate that all these things we have described are taken care of by the body's marvelous automatic machinery. If we had to control consciously all the details of processing our food in its journey through our bodies, the result would surely be confusion, and perhaps worse. But all these things happen with no thought on our part. In fact, most of them happen in our total ignorance of what is going on. This is unfortunate, for some knowledge of the digestive and energy-conversion processes might make us wiser eaters and better caretakers of our precious and priceless bodies.

CHAPTER
4

The Basic Foodstuffs

It has been recommended by the National Academy of Sciences-National Research Council in the United States that the average food intake be held to about 2,700 calories per day. This translates into about 1½ pounds of food. Now, a slice of bread has about 65 calories, and a 40-slice loaf would just about meet the 2,700 calorie requirement. Thus the poet's "loaf of bread, jug of wine, and thou" would seem to take care of one's needs for nutrition. However, although bread has been well named the "staff of life," we need more than that to be adequately nourished, as is obvious where people are fed mainly on cereal grains. Variety is more than the spice of life; it is a nutritional necessity. We need not only the carbohydrates in which bread abounds but proteins, fats, minerals, and vitamins besides. Bread often does not provide all these in the proper amounts.

As we noted in Chapter 1, a calorie is a measure of heat energy, or food energy. One "small" calorie is enough energy to raise the temperature of one cubic centimeter of water one degree Centigrade. A "kilocalorie" or 1000 small calories, raises the temperature of about a half-gallon of water one degree Centigrade. This kilocalorie is the calorie that nutritionists use in describing food energy.

There are calories and there are other calories. Carbohydrates produce about 4 calories per gram of weight; a pound of starch contains some 1,500 calories. Not surprisingly, a gram of fat yields 9 calories. Protein matches the caloric value of carbohydrates. Each of these components has its place in diet and we need a proper balance of all three, plus small amounts of minerals and vitamins to keep our bodies in good condition. Since carbohydrates are the simplest of the foods, we'll begin our discussion with them.

CARBOHYDRATES

When a plant leaf puts carbon, hydrogen and oxygen together it makes a carbohydrate. There are a number of these: glucose, fructose, maltose, lactose, sucrose, glycogen, dextrin, starch, and cellulose. Grouped more simply, there are sugars, starches, and cellulose. The body uses them all and absorbs about 97 percent of carbohydrates on the average, although man cannot properly digest cellulose and its only purpose is for "roughage" to aid in the digestive process.

Sugar is the basic carbohydrate. It is easily soluble in water and easily digested. Starches are less soluble and form a paste, as we know from having made library paste from cornstarch and water. The celluloses are not soluble at all. However, starch and cellulose may both be degraded to the basic sugar form in the laboratory and also in some animals' digestive processes.

Carbohydrates may also be considered as three groups of sugars: *monosaccharides,* the simple sugars that cannot be broken down into more basic units; *disaccharides,* containing up to five molecules of simple or compound forms of sugar; and *polysaccharides,* the large aggregates of complex forms of sugar.

The monosaccharides include fruits, honey, and corn syrup. We get about 5 percent of our carbohydrates from these *glucoses* and *fructoses* in the United States.

Disaccharides, not quite as digestible, include cane and beet sugars, molasses, maple syrup, milk, and milk products. About 10 percent of our carbohydrates come from the lactose in milk and milk products, and 25 percent from the sucrose in sugars and syrups.

About 50 percent of our carbohydrates come from polysaccharides, or starches in grains and vegetables. The polysaccharide glycogen is found in meat products and seafood, but this represents a negligible amount in our diet. About 5 percent of our carbohydrate diet is made up of the indigestible sugars, from such sources as cellulose stalks, leaves, outer covering of seeds, and partially digestible plants, such as artichokes, onions, and garlic.

Sugar is the "quick-energy" food because it is in a form requiring little further change to be used as heat or energy in the body. Candy and other sweets are well known for supplying quick satisfaction, and that is probably why sweets are so popular with most people the world over.

We could live on carbohydrates if all the body needed was heat and energy, for they are excellent sources of energy. Unfortunately, many people eat far too much sugar and starch, either because they have no choice or because they do not know the nutritional weakness of such foods.

Fats (called *lipids* in scientific terminology) are also high-energy foods and yield about 9 calories per gram, more than twice as much as carbohydrates and proteins. They are *esters,* or compounds, of fatty acids, and generally separated by type into *fats* from animal sources and *oils* from vegetables. There are three kinds of fatty acids known to be required in human diet: *linoleic, linolenic,* and *arachidonic.* There are also *glycolipids,* which contain carbohydrates, and *lipo-proteins,* or fat-protein combinations.

Because oil and water don't mix, fats are insoluble in water but can be dissolved by organic solvents. They are very complex in structure, formed of long-linked chains of carbon and hydrogen. Like carbohydrates, the fats vary in complexity, and there seem to be some differences in the various types with respect to nutrition. Simple fats have chains of carbon atoms, all surrounded by hydrogen atoms.

In some fats, as we said in Chapter 1, there are occasional adjacent "missing links" between carbon and hydrogen atoms. Such fats are called *monounsaturates.* When there are many vacancies instead of carbon-hydrogen links the fats are *polyunsaturates.* Much heart trouble is believed caused by too much cholesterol in the blood vessels, and experiments seem to indicate that the polyunsaturate fats lower this cholesterol level. Recently there has been a great deal of publicity in this regard, and vegetable oils and fish oils are highly regarded as substitutes for animal fats. Safflower, for example, enjoyed a sudden popularity when its oil was found to be very low in saturates. However, the Food and Drug Administration feels that labeling fat-containing products such as margarines and cooking

The Basic Foodstuffs • 45

oils serves no useful purpose for the consumer and forbids describing polyunsaturates as beneficial in the prevention and treatment of diseases of the heart and circulatory system. Doctors recommend generally that we reduce our consumption of all fats as a precaution against heart and vein disorders.

Fats produce layers under the skin that protect against loss of heat and are also the stockpiles we draw on when food is not available. A certain amount of fat is necessary and helps to shape the body attractively. However, excess fat builds up in certain areas of the body to produce the "spare tire" and other unsightly lumpiness. Fat is called adipose tissue.

Safflower, relatively unfamiliar to most Americans before the concern for cutting down on saturated fats, is increasingly popular as a source of cooking oil. Photo by Harold Wylie, College of Agriculture Photo, U. of Arizona.

Body fat is not static in the body but has a turnover of 10 percent a day.

When we eat more than we need for energy and body maintenance, the surplus is stored as fat. Some physiologists believe, however, that there are individuals whose metabolism produces excess fat even from a relatively small intake. On the other hand, there is the disease called *cachexia* that occurs when infection, cancer, diabetes, or other such ills diminish the store of fat and cause emaciation or wasting away of the tissues.

Fats prolong the time that foods remain in the stomach and thus stave off hunger. They are, however, highly digestible; about 95 percent of fat is absorbed into the body. Fats and oils help to carry the fat-soluble vitamins A and D from the digestive system into the bloodstream and are the chief sources of Vitamin E. The body also depends on the fats for vitamin K absorption. In the United States fat consumption has increased appreciably over the last few decades, and fat now represents about 40 percent of our diet, coming mostly from meat, fish, poultry, milk, butter, and the oils used for salads and cooking. Fried foods are very popular with many peoples, and food fried in animal or vegetable fats (or oils) are tastier, higher in calories, and have additional vitamins. Unless foods are overcooked in them, cooking fats and oils should not materially hinder the digestibility of the foods.

PROTEINS

Proteins are the most complex of the food elements. Fats consist of linked carbon and hydrogen molecules; carbohydrates have carbon, hydrogen, and oxygen; and proteins have all three, plus nitrogen. In addition, proteins generally contain sulfur. Many contain phosphorus, with copper, iodine, iron, and zinc occasionally present. In view of their complexity of structure, it is not surprising that proteins are the hardest foods to digest. On the average, only 92 percent of the protein in food is absorbed by the body.

Proteins are equal to carbohydrates in calories and can be used, as carbohydrates and fats are used, for the production of heat and energy. But the main function of proteins is the building and maintenance of our bodies. They are the very "stuff of life," and the gene, or blueprint of life, is a giant molecule of protein. All of our tissues, skin, muscle, blood, bone, and so on, are proteins, and this is why it is said that we are what we eat. We are made of the protein building blocks in our diet.

Scientists suspected long ago that proteins were substances very different from other constituents of the body and other foods. The French chemist Pierre Macquer in 1777 coined the term *albuminous* for these substances, which strangely solidified when heated. Albumen was the Latin name for egg white, and egg white, casein, and globulin from blood were among the albuminous substances.

By 1820 a French chemist named M. H. Braconnot had heated gelatin in acid and produced a sweet-tasting crystalline substance. He named this *glycine,* from the Greek word for sweet. The "ine" ending indicated that the compound contained nitrogen. Shortly thereafter, Braconnot isolated a white crystalline substance from muscle tissue. This was named *leucine* from the Greek word for white. Glycine and leucine were amino acids, made up of ammonia-containing groups and carboxylic acid groups of atoms. Although Braconnot did not know it, these are the building blocks of protein.

In 1839 a Dutch chemist named Gerardus Mulder analyzed and wrote a chemical formula for the basic albuminous substance. The formula was $C_{40}H_{62}O_{12}N_{10}$, but Mulder gave it a name that was easier to say—*protein*—from the Greek word *proteios,* meaning "of first importance." Whether Mulder knew it or not, this was a most fitting name, since protein is indeed of first importance.

The German chemist Justus von Liebig soon proved that proteins were of even greater importance in the diet than carbohydrates and fats. He also isolated the amino acid *tyrosine* from milk, naming it for the Greek word for cheese. Von Liebig's great work in the field makes it easy for us to forgive his mistake in believing that plants took nitrogen in from the air instead of through the soil.

Proteins are made up of 22 amino acids, although fortunately man is able to manage with only 8 "essential" aminos in his food. These are:

tryptophan	valine
phenylalanine	methionine
lysine	leucine
threonine	isoleucine

Tests have shown that for a man the following amounts of additional amino acids daily are desirable:

trypotophan	0.5 (grams)
phenylalanine	2.2
lysine	1.6
threonine	1.0
valine	1.6
methionine	2.2
leucine	2.2
isoleucine	1.4

The "nonessential," or "dispensable," aminos for man are:

glycine	proline
alanine	hydroxyproline
arginine	histidine
serine	citruline
aspartic acid	cystine
glutamic acid	tyrosine

Classifying certain aminos as nonessential does not mean that the body does not require them for growth and maintenance. Quite the contrary; we need these amino acids too, but if there is sufficient nitrogen in the diet in other constituents, the body can manufacture the missing aminos—even those whose names we find it difficult to spell!

One gram of protein does not necessarily equal another gram. Some is more readily available for use by the body. For instance, animal protein is generally better from a biological, or nutritional, standpoint than vegetable protein. This is because the animal has further refined the proteins from its plant diet. Man is an animal too, and thus the protein from animal tissue is better matched to his food needs.

In 1854 the first work on differences in value of proteins in various foods was done at Rothamsted Station in England. More recently the Food and Agriculture Organization of the United Nations, long active in nutritional studies, has set up a standard of values for protein. Egg is considered the best protein source and is rated at 100. Following are some representative protein foods with their comparative ratings.

Net Protein Utilization*

fish	83
meat	82
milk	75
cheese	75
potatoes	71
cassava	71
fruits	70
vegetables	70
cereals	56
peanuts	48
pulses	46

*A measure of the digestibility of protein and the biologic value of its amino acid mixture absorbed from the intestine.

Net Protein Utilization, or NPU, is not the full story, of course. Quantity, like quality, is important. Cassava flour, used by many of the world's peoples, is less than 2 percent protein. Wheat flour, at about 10 percent, is much better. Potatoes, which have a fairly high quality of protein, are also only about 10 percent protein. Corn is about the same, but rice is only 8 percent. On the other hand, milk is 20 percent protein, soybean seed is 36 percent, and lean fish more than 37 percent.

The United States Department of Agriculture suggests the intake of 60 grams of protein a day per person. The United Nations Food and Agriculture Organization recommends 75 grams daily. These figures represent about 10 to 12 percent of total food intake by weight. Furthermore, from 10 to 15 percent of the protein should be animal protein.

If we were faced with a choice of eating all proteins, all carbohydrates, or all fats, proteins would be best, since they serve every nutritional function. However, a mixture of the three, plus vitamins and minerals, is preferable.

When the diet consists mostly of proteins, all of the amino acids are not required for body-building, of course. In this case, the excess amino acids are broken down by removing the nitrogen from them. The residue is then burned up, along with fats and carbohydrates, for energy and heat.

Because protein is the source of growth, it is recommended that infants up to one year of age be provided with 3.5 grams of protein for each kilogram (2.2 pounds) of body weight. Growing children and expectant or nursing mothers should have from 1.5 to 2.0 grams of protein per kilogram of body weight, and the rest of us need about one gram per kilogram. An average male weighing about 165 pounds (75 Kg.) requires a protein intake of about 70 grams daily, or about 10 percent of his total food consumption. Any amount over that will be used, as we have noted, for energy or fat production.

We need additional protein in our diet during and following an illness, so that new tissue can be produced to replace losses. During starvation the liver loses most of the protein lost by the body. Next comes the alimentary tract, then the pancreas and the spleen, followed by the heart, muscles, skin, bones, and finally the brain, which conserves its protein most efficiently of all. The average half-life of total body protein is about eighty days. But since the liver and "serum," or bloodstream, protein has a half-life of only about ten days, this allows the lung, brain, bone, skin, and muscle to average 158 days.

Since proteins are hard to digest, many of our protein foods are cooked before eating. Meats are a prime example. It is possible to eat raw meat, although it should at least be chopped fine to aid in digestion. Many people eat other protein foods raw, for example oysters and some fish, since they are soft and digestible in this state.

THE MINERALS

We have considered the nutrients that are important in bulk, the carbohydrates, fats, and proteins. These we must have in quantities of several hundred grams daily. There are other nutrients we need only to the extent of thousandths, or even millionths, of grams daily. These *micronutrients* include minerals and vitamins. We will discuss the minerals first.

At the turn of the last century, a United States Department of Agriculture scientist named C. F. Langworthy set down much of what was then known about the subject in ten "Laws of Nutrition." His fourth point was that "A certain amount of food material, i.e., protein, fat, and carbohydrates, is required for maintenance. Mineral is also essential, but very little is known regarding the kind and amount necessary." In the seventy years that have followed we have learned much about these essential minerals.

While all the other nutrients are organic or carbon-containing compounds, minerals are inorganic. Most of our diet is water, for food is made up largely of this compound. We drink about two pounds of water daily and get much more in our food. About 70 percent of our body weight (less fat) is water.

Water is classified as a mineral. There are a number of other minerals we need, although not in the quantities we require of water. There are seventeen of these minerals that nutritionists know we require. Some are needed in greater quantities. They include calcium, chlorine, iron, magnesium, phosphorus, potassium, sodium and sulfur. Also needed, but only in "trace" amounts of a few millionths of an ounce, are chromium, cobalt, copper, fluorine, iodine, manganese, molybdenum, selenium, zinc, and perhaps vanadium. There do not seem to be any of the so-called "precious" metals, like gold, in our bodies, but those that are there are often precious to our health. Lack of iodine, for example, can cause goiter, and for this reason most table salt sold today is "iodized" so that there will be sufficient iodine for good health. Copper is necessary for proper use of iron in the blood. Minerals are vital to proper development and maintenance of bones and teeth.

THE VITAMINS

Langworthy's "Laws of Nutrition" admitted a lack of knowledge of minerals. Vitamins were not even mentioned, for nutritionists were almost completely ignorant of these very important micronutrients that nature generally makes available to man. When they were not available, of course, the results were often tragic.

F. G. Hopkins in 1906 established the fact that in addition to carbohydrates, fats, proteins, water and minerals, food contained other substances, which he called "accessory food factors." The name "vitamin" was coined in 1913 by a scientist named Casimir Funk, who was working on the mystery of these unknown accessory factors that apparently were very important in diet. Many of the amino acids were known by this time, and Funk decided to call the factors "vital amines," or "vitamines." When it was learned later that not all were actually amines, the "e" was dropped.

Funk established the concept of "deficiency diseases," for those caused by the lack of some vital constituent in the diet. We consume vitamins in such tiny quantities that they would be hard to see, yet without them men sicken and sometimes die. In fact, it was just such tragedies that led to the discovery of vitamins and the consequent improvement of our diets by their addition where needed.

Long before Casimir Funk's time, before there was any concept of nutrition in a formal sense, men knew that certain foods and substances seemed to cure illnesses of certain kinds. North American Indians demonstrated to French explorers suffering from scurvy that eating an extract of spruce needles would help them back to health. Spruce needles happen to be rich in Vitamin C, but neither the Indians nor the French could know that. Men simply learned by trial and error that some remedies helped.

A pioneer in vitamin detective work was a doctor in the Royal Navy named James Lind. In 1747 Lind treated a dozen men for scurvy by feeding them various items in addition to their regular diet. He experimented with such "medicines" as sea water, sulfuric acid, garlic, and even balsam, a tree resin. The resin did not have the effect the spruce needles had, and not until Lind tried oranges and lemons on the ailing men did he achieve success. But when they were given citrus fruits, the men ate them "with greediness." This was a hopeful sign, and almost at once Lind's patients improved. Ironically, it took almost fifty years because of red tape, but eventually the Royal Navy adopted the practice of requiring citrus fruit in the diet of its sailors. Because the English called lemons "limes" they acquired the nickname of "Limeys," and a whole section of the London docks became known as "Limehouse."

Lind had not isolated the real problem, of course. Citrus fruits and green vegetables "cured" scurvy, and so they were considered medicines instead of required foods for a proper diet. In 1907 an American college professor named Verner McCollum, who as a baby had been cured of scurvy by eating apple peelings, began to seek the basis of nutritional value in food. McCollum seems to have been the first researcher to use rats in his experiments. He did so because of their short life cycle. Why wait years for results when rats provided it in weeks? he asked. By 1912 he and his

A Malawi mother, benefiting from nutritional information learned in FAO'S community health programs, gives her baby his daily orange juice. FAO Photo by F. Botts.

coworkers had isolated a substance present in small quantities in certain fats, in alfalfa, and in the livers and kidney of some animals. He called this substance "fat-soluble A" (Funk had not yet thought up the name vitamin). Later McCollum discovered vitamin D, which prevents the bone disease called rickets. By 1948 all thirteen vitamins known to be necessary in the human diet had been identified. Among them was vitamin C, which prevents scurvy; thiamine, which prevents *beri-beri;* and niacin, which prevents pellagra. Ironically, niacin had been synthesized in 1867 from pyridine by chemists, but its importance to health was not realized for decades.

Albert Szent-Gyorgi first isolated Vitamin C in Hungarian paprika. Vitamins are where you find them. Centuries ago the Scots knew about cod-liver oil as a cure for the bone disease called rickets. Cod-liver oil is rich in vitamin D. The body synthesizes this vitamin in sunshine, but in countries short of sunlight the vitamin is necessary in the diet. However, overdoses of vitamin D can cause nausea, loss of appetite, kidney damage, and calcium deposits in tissues.

One problem that made work with vitamins so difficult was that few medical men and scientists could conceive of a disease caused by the *lack* of something. It was well known that germs cause disease, but how could the absence of something cause a similar condition? This argument raged over research in the disease beriberi and made it most difficult to establish the simple fact that feeding beriberi victims the husks from the polished rice that "made them sick" made them well again! And this same controversy delayed acceptance of the theory that diet deficiency caused the killing disease pellagra. For years, most authorities continued to hold to the erroneous view that germs must cause pellagra, just as they caused other diseases. Rickets, they claimed, was caused not by a vitamin D deficiency, but by too little sun, too much rain, or some other factor.

Vitamins and minerals are lost in cooking, mainly in the water used in the process. If possible this water should be eaten with the vegetables or meat cooked in it to recapture the value. During studies of pellagra sufferers in the South, it was found that, oddly, the very poor did not suffer as much as those better off financially. The more prosperous were throwing away the "pot likker" from their cooked food, while the poor people were eating it! Now we know that it is wise to cook with as little water as necessary and save the nutritious juices or broth.

We have mentioned that fats are carriers of the fat-soluble vitamins A, D, E, and K. There are also water-soluble vitamins. The complete list of vitamins, their sources, and uses, follows:

Vitamin (Fat Soluble)	*Source*	*Purpose*
A	Fish-liver oils green plants, carrots	Needed for growth and longevity; eyesight

Vitamin (Fat Soluble)	Source	Purpose
D	Fish oils	Guards against ricketts, a bone disease
E	Grain and vegetable oils	Protects vitamin A
K	Green vegetables	Assures clotting of blood in bleeding, aids liver
(Water-Soluble)		
B (thiamine)	Pork, liver, whole grains	Guards against beri-beri, heart disease
Riboflavin	Milk, egg white, leafy vegetables	healthy skin
Niacin	Yeast, wheat germ, meats	Guards against pellagra
Pantothenic acid	Liver, kidneys, green vegetables, egg yolk	metabolic processes
B	Whole grains, liver yeast, egg yolk	Blood and skin metabolism
Biotin	Liver, kidney, yeast	Needed for growth
Folic Acid	Liver, deep green leafy vegetables,	Guards against anemia
B	Liver, meats	Guards against pernicious anemia
Vitamin C	Citrus fruit, fresh vegetables, potatoes	Guards against scurvy

It is doubtful that men of science have yet learned all there is to know about nutrition and the prevention of disease through proper diet. Quite probably additions will continue to be made to the list as man discovers new things about what he eats.

Total vitamin consumption is less than 200 milligrams daily. Vitamin B_{12}, the most recently discovered vitamin, is required in quantities of only 140 *billionths* of an ounce each day! Yet shortages of even this tiny amount can lead to ill health. Vitamin deficiencies kill countless people each year. For this reason the discovery of vitamins was of great importance. Now it is possible to manufacture vitamins commercially and add them to foods at the factory so that we will have sufficient vitamins in our diet. Apparently vitamins are vitamins, whether they are produced by bacteria in the intestines, by plants, or by a pharmaceutical laboratory.

THE PROPER DIET

Beyond carbohydrates, fats, and proteins, nutritionists knew little about food values before 1900, but the pace picked up shortly thereafter. In 1960 Dr. McCollum, who had discovered the first vitamin in 1912, listed a total of 47 nutrients, including 17 vitamins, and pointed out that these had been discovered or isolated at an average rate of about one a year. Adding to these all the many seasonings man has a taste for and the thousands of varieties of food, we can see that nutrition is a complex process. Yet there are simple rules and guidelines that can help preserve the natural checks and balances built into our bodies. The National Academy of Sciences—National Research Council recommends the following dietary intakes for various persons of average weight and height:

	Age	Caloric Intake	Proteins (Grams)
Children	6 to 9	2,100	52
Boys	15 to 18	3,400	85
Girls	15 to 18	2,300	58
Men	18 to 35	2,900	70
Women	18 to 35	2,100	58

It is also desirable that about a fifth of the protein be animal protein, which is of high biological quality. Of course a person doing strenuous physical work will require more calories than one sitting at a desk or lying in bed. It was once thought that those living in cold countries needed more calories to produce needed heat, but more recently there has been a belief that more food may be needed in the tropics because of the effects of heat.

CHAPTER
5

Meat: A Luxury Food?

There are many interesting comments in the Bible on the relative values of plant food and meat. In the Book of *Genesis* the first sons of Adam and Eve are described:

> . . . And Abel was a keeper of sheep, but Cain was a tiller of the ground.
> And in the process of time it came to pass, that Cain brought of the fruit of the ground an offering unto the Lord. And Abel, he also brought of the firstlings of his flock and of the fat thereof. And the Lord had respect unto Abel and to his offering.
> But unto Cain and to his offering he had not respect . . ."

The expression "fat of the land" refers to fat meat, and the prodigal son was welcomed back with a "fatted calf," indicating that ancient peoples thought of meat as a luxury food. Today it still is, for many of the world's people.

Before men turned to farming, the food supply was broad and varied, consisting of meat, fish, milk, milk products, and eggs, supplemented with wild grains and vegetables, fruits and nuts. By working an area of land diligently, a small number of humans could provide themselves with sufficient and nourishing food. This was a "natural" diet, and it suffered with the coming of farming.

Ironically, the shortage of meat is the price the world had to pay for agriculture. Farming made it possible for the land to feed many more people. Now there are so many of us to be fed that grain and vegetables must suffice for most. This is unfortunate, for meat contains the nutrients to satisfy man's need for high-quality protein, rich in the amino acids we need for proper body maintenance and growth. Back during the days of hunting and gathering, men probably ate more meat than they eat now, and animals were domesticated long before men began to farm. However, we cannot appropriately say it is unfortunate that the world turned to farming, for without agriculture most of us could not be fed. And surely most of us would rather have a meat-short menu than no menu at all.

MAN, THE HUNTER

From much research, including the archaeological diggings around old caves or settlements that unearth animal bones, we know that for tens of thousands of years men caught wild animals for food. Even if we did not know this for a fact, it would be easy to guess that they had, because so many of us still have a love for hunting or fishing, or both, deep within us. This recurrence in an organism of something tracing back to distant ancestors is called "atavism." Some writers suggest that our word "game" comes from man's first sport, that of hunting game animals. Atavism is said to account also for the good feeling of sitting by the campfire.

Some rugged and healthy peoples, including Australian aborigines, Eskimos, and tribes of Masai warriors in Africa, still subsist largely on meat and fish. The Masai get practically all their nourishment from cattle they herd on the eastern grasslands of Africa. About a fourth of their needs are satisfied by this meat, which they supplement with as much as a gallon of milk a day and some fruit. At certain times they also draw blood from the jugular veins of cattle and drink it plain or mixed with milk. Nutritionists wonder that the Masai do not suffer from heart trouble, but they are among the strongest people in the world. Their young men are capable of walking sixty miles a day and running faster than Americans who have a more "nutritious" diet.

Some researchers believe that early man caught small game with his hands, or with the help of sticks and rocks, almost from the time he appeared on earth. Perhaps 400,000 years ago men learned to fashion crude spears and clubs or axes. The use of these weapons, coupled with the harnessing of fire, made it possible for hunters in packs to go after larger game, which could be cooked if desired. Gradually the techniques improved, and there is evidence of man's use of effective knives and a variety of pits and traps for catching animals some 75,000 years ago. Long before the cultivation of crops, men had weapons and tools. Man's first tools may have been imitations of animal claws or tusks, or quite probably those claws and tusks themselves. In time an arsenal of weapons was developed, including clubs, knives, spears, bows and arrows, lassos, bolas, boomerangs, slingshots, stones, traps, snares, and lures.

Man must also have learned from animals the wisdom of storing up food against hunger. Dogs he befriended buried bones, bees made honey, and the ants stored food for "rainy days." In primeval times man had to eat his catch quickly to prevent spoiling. With the coming of fire and cooking, he learned to preserve it for short periods of time. Later, sun drying, curing, and smoking processed a food that could be kept a long time even though it was not so longlasting as grains.

THE KEEPERS OF SHEEP

One theory, which appears reasonable, is that domestication of animals came about from the capturing of small ones for pets, perhaps for children. Some species would soon outgrow their pleasing tame ways and have to be killed or set free. But others remained tame, and their masters could see the advantages of keeping them for a supply of milk and meat. Gradually the practice of breeding a pair of animals into a herd came into being. Abel and his brothers became shepherds and herdsmen.

In 1951 archaeologists excavated two ancient settlements in northern Iraq. These were Shanidar Cave, a rather small natural cave that sheltered perhaps thirty people, and Zawi Chemi Shanidar, a valley village or camp not far away. It was obvious that these people had begun to domesticate animals, particularly sheep, by about 9,000 B.C. Goats, too, were used for food, but the sheep is a better animal for this purpose. As man became more advanced he sought to please his palate with choicer meats.

There is a good reason why sheep were the first domesticated food animal. Sheep are sizable creatures and probably kept the early herders busy tending them. But they are generally docile. The more difficult animals were domesticated after man had gained experience with sheep. It is believed that goats were added to the family by about 7,000 B.C. Not until long after that were cattle tamed.

AND OTHER ANIMALS

Bos primigenius, the aurochs, from which came all our domesticated cattle—and from which we also got the name "Bossy," by the way—was a huge animal, sometimes seven feet high at the shoulders, and with long, wickedly curled horns. And the aurochs had little desire to be a friend and beefsteak to man. The sheep, the dog, and even the horse were fairly easy to domesticate, but it took much more effort with the aurochs. Nevertheless, about 5,000 B.C., some brave herders began the task of selecting the less ferocious of the *Bos primigenius* and turning them into walking meat larders and dairy animals.

Although the last aurochs died in captivity in Poland in 1627, geneticists have been able to "work in reverse" from existing animals and breed back to the aurochs! Such a biological throwback was for scientific purposes only, for the aurochs would be no match for today's specialized and productive cattle breeds we depend on for meat and milk.

Of the many species of animals in the world, man uses only a few for the production of meat for his table. Beef, the most popular, provides about 50 percent of the total world meat supply. Next is pork, representing about 40 percent of the total. Lamb, mutton, and goat account for about 8 percent. Buffalo, camel, and horsemeat are also eaten, but these meats represent a minor portion of the total.

Deer, rabbit, kangaroo, antelope, and other wild game are eaten to some extent, and some rabbit meat is produced commercially or for subsistence by individuals.

In ancient times cannibalism was widespread, and captives were often eaten as food. Superstition held that by eating a man one acquired his wisdom and virility. Some cannibals prized the meat of white men, a delicacy they called "long pig." While there are still scattered occurrences of cannibalism, and in times of starvation men may turn to it in

Meat: A Luxury Food • 61

desperation, the practice is abhorrent to civilized peoples, and human flesh is no longer a staple commodity.

FOWL FOR FOOD

Men stole eggs from birds' nests and caught and ate the birds themselves, when they could, far back in time. Birds were caught and drowned by underwater swimmers, or by tying kernels of grain to string and setting them out as bait, as one would for fish. It was not surprising that about 1,500 B.C., men began to domesticate fowl, probably beginning with wild turkeys.

Although a great variety of birds are consumed for meat, including doves, pheasants, quail, ducks, and pigeons, most of our fowl food consists of chickens and turkeys. Broilers, raised in a production-line environment, are the most important and perhaps the most efficiently produced meat.

Eggs, a very fine food, are important in our diet and are consumed in large quantities in the United States. They are eaten alone or combined with other foods in cakes and other pastries, meat loaf, and casseroles.

Egg candling (the time-honored method for finding fertilized eggs) in the Poultry Department of the University of Arizona Experiment Station at Tucson. Photo by John Burnham, U. of Arizona.

ANIMAL PRODUCTS

Blood was undoubtedly highly prized by primitive humans who ate it right at the kill as animals do, ripping open the jugular vein of their prey to slake both hunger and thirst. Today only the Masai and a few other primitive peoples drink blood this way, and most meat animals are bled before processing. But another primitive practice has been developed to a high science. The Masai themselves consume far more milk than blood.

Milk, as it obvious by its use for young children, is the perfect food, whether it be mother's milk, or milk from a cow, a mare, or a goat. Most of us depend on dairy cows rather than mares or goats today, although these other animals satisfy some diets. The good thing about milk is that a productive dairy animal provides a neverfailing supply of it for many years.

Milk is the basic dairy product. From it comes a variety of cheeses, including cottage cheese. Cream and butter also are milk foods, high in fat and in protein. Yogurt, made as a culture by adding two kinds of bacteria, is popular with some central European peoples and with many health food fans in this country.

Primitive herdsmen learned to milk their domestic animals many thousands of years ago, and we have leaned heavily on this animal product for food ever since. Cows produce more than 90 percent of the world's milk total, the rest coming from goats, sheep, deer, buffalo, camels, donkeys, mares, and yaks.

Without refrigeration, milk does not keep long, and it must be consumed in the developing countries on a day to day basis. For this reason it is often made into cheese, a product that keeps for long periods of time.

Legend has it that cheese was discovered quite by accident. Long ago, according to the story, an Arabian merchant put some milk in a pouch made from a sheep's stomach. He slung this over his camel and set out on a long journey across the hot desert. By nightfall the milk understandably had curdled from the heat, and also because of the *rennet,* a digestive enzyme in the sheep's stomach lining. The merchant drank and enjoyed the whey, or liquid portion, and found that the solidified curds, or cheese, was an even greater pleasure; and so cheese-making was added to man's food production methods. This was an estimated 4,000 years ago. Today there are hundreds of kinds of cheeses made all over the world. Even whey, the watery remains from cheese-making, generally discarded for lack of a

Stainless steel automated machines churn cream into butter granules, remove buttermilk, wash and press the granules together to form butter, then salt and package the butter. After the day's run, an automated cleaning system takes over. U.S. Department of Agriculture Photo.

use for it, has been turned into a delicious and inexpensive high-protein drink by researchers.

Butter is another form of milk. It does not keep as well as cheese and must be kept cool. We know that it has been made for at least 4,000 years, because the people of India were using it 2,000 years before Christ. They were first to use the twirling churn. Clarified butter, or *ghee,* made by heating butter in a vat to remove the water, is popular in India, as we know from the story of Little Black Sambo and the tigers who melted into ghee. It is also used in other Asian countries, in Arab countries, and in Africa for cooking.

There are many other milk products in common use, including:

    Buttermilk   Evaporated milk
    Cream   Condensed milk
    Sour Cream   Filled milk
    Yogurt   Clabber
    Skim milk

64 • FEAST AND FAMINE

Milk is about 87 percent water. Of the dry matter, 30 percent is fat, 27 percent protein, 37 percent lactose (carbohydrate), and about 5 percent minerals. Thus milk contains all of the needed constituents. Not surprisingly, Americans drink almost a quart of milk a day on the average.

FOOD FROM THE SEA

Men must have first caught fish with their bare hands when the creatures became stranded in pools or on beaches. Later they learned to club or spear them, and finally the techniques of hook and net were evolved. From fragments of bone or stone hooks and "gorges," we know that men were fishers tens of thousands of years ago. It is interesting to think of an ancient hook-maker laboriously drilling a hole in a stone and then carefully cutting a perfectly curved hook from around the hole. Man probably wove nets before he wove cloth. Polynesian fishermen reputedly used nets thousands of feet long, requiring a hundred men to handle them.

Mesolithic and Neolithic fish-hooks. (a) Maglemosian; the fish shows a possible method of securing bait; (b) Natufian, bone; (c) Tasian, shell or horn.

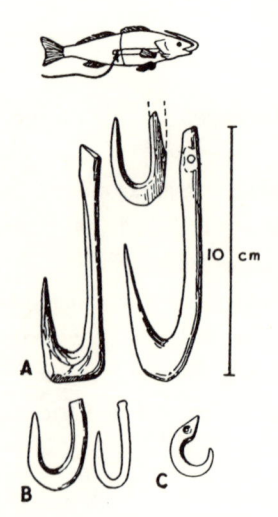

Netting and curing fish in Saqqara, Egypt, c 2500 B.C. Illustrations from *A History of Technology* (Singer et al, Oxford University Press)

Other clever methods of catching fish included putting narcotics or intoxicants into the water to stupefy the fish for easy catching.

Man has been a fisherman perhaps as long or longer than he has hunted animals on land, but worldwide he does not consume as much fish as meat, despite the love of many for fishing as a sport. Large quantities of seafoods are consumed only in those countries in which meat is unavailable and fish is plentiful. There are island and seacoast cultures that depend almost entirely on the sea for their food, just as their ancestors have done for thousands of years. Japan, one of the most advanced countries, consumes great quantities of fish, since Japanese farmlands cannot support enough livestock to supply meat for all.

About 90 percent of the world's fish catch comes from the ocean.

In Dahomey, where this kind of lagoon fishing has declined, FAO has introduced outboard motors, capsize-proof launching gear, and specially designed vessels for reaching previously inaccessible offshore fishing areas. FAO Photo by G. Tortoli.

Jim Sallee tosses food pellets to rainbow trout at the Willow Beach Fish Hatchery in Arizona. Bureau of Commercial Fisheries Photo.

This supply may be divided into the two broad categories of *demersal,* or bottom fish, and *pelagic,* or surface-swimming fish. Of the 20,000 or so species of fish man uses only a few dozen, just as he has concentrated on only a few of the plant species for food.

Herring, menhaden, sardines, anchovies and other *clupeoids* make up about 33 percent of the world's fish catch. While many of these are eaten, a great deal of fish oil is also produced from them by the process of reduction.

The next most important fish commercially include the cod, haddock, hake, and related species, all bottom fish, which have long been standard items on many menus and make up about 12 percent of the world catch.

Sea bass, mullets, perch, croaker, and similar fish are the next group in size of catch, making about 10 percent of the total. Next in importance are tuna, mackerel, flounder, salmon, trout and smelt. Less caught but still used by some people as food are sharks and rays of various types.

Whales (although not to be classed as fish) provide food, along with many other products. Men have long gone to sea for the whale, harpooning it by hand from small boats and risking their lives in the ensuing battle when the giant mammals fought back for their lives. But with modern technology the harpoon gun came into being, and now whales are shot with powerful weapons that kill them instantly. Air pumped into the whale keeps it afloat, and a huge "factory ship" processes the many thousands of pounds of meat and other products. So effective are new whaling techniques that whales are in danger of becoming extinct.

Shellfish, including oysters, clams, abalone, squid, octopus, (which are molluscs) and shrimp, lobster, and crab (which are crustaceans) are also taken by the millions of tons each year.

Ten percent of the marine harvest comes from fresh water, including rivers, lakes, ponds and even reservoirs. For centuries, and perhaps even thousands of years, men have "farmed" fish in ponds, even in cultivated fields. In ancient times the Romans "farmed" oysters, even building huge jetties to protect them from the sea storms that crashed against the shore. The Chinese and Javanese grew fish in ponds, as did the Hawaiians of early times. These techniques persist today in Japan, Spain, France, Taiwan, and elsewhere, and fish and shellfish farming promises to become a source of increasing amounts of healthful protein food. This is easily understandable when we consider that it is possible to raise tons of oysters a year in an acre of water, and that their food comes largely from the water and costs nothing.

The raising of fish in rice paddies, especially the plant-eating *bango* or milkfish, is typical of clever ways of increasing the yield of food. Fish are also raised in reservoirs, some of which are fertilized to produce more fish. In Japan, trout grown in "raceways" produce fantastic yields per acre of land (although of course much water is circulated through the raceways).

British scientists are experimenting with feeding fish supplemental food in the lochs of Scotland and growing fish in the warmed waste water from nuclear power plants. These practices show promise, although an extension of the idea to fertilizing the ocean seems doomed to failure. It has been calculated that, unfortunately, the return in fish would repay only a small fraction of the cost of fertilizing the open sea.

Plants, including seaweed and algae, grow in the sea, of course. Both of these are used to a small extent, particularly by the Japanese, who "mow" the beds of seaweed and use the crop for food plus a number of drugs and other uses as well. Smaller algae, too, is used as food, but it has not lived up to expectations, since it is poor in taste and costs more to produce than equally nutritious and better-accepted products of other kinds.

One way to meet the problem of protein shortages in some lands is to turn fish into Fish Protein Concentrate, or FPC, a rich and nutritious flour that would supply protein needs for a few pennies a day per person. However, people have not as yet accepted this food product, and it will probably take a good "selling" job before it finds a commercially profitable place in foods as an additive.

THE HIGH COST OF MEAT

The animal population is huge. There are more than a billion cattle in the world, half a billion hogs, and a billion sheep, and added to this are several billion chickens and turkeys. Thus the population of animals we raise for food exceeds our human population considerably—as we should expect from the law of tithes! Some authorities have estimated that the biomass of meat animals is equivalent to about 15 billion humans. Thus the world is already supporting the equivalent of 18.5 billion humans, instead of the 3.5 billion we generally consider.

These are meat animals only. When we add the population of our pets, which is sizable, and of wild animals, the figure must be far greater even than the 15 billion human-equivalents mentioned above.

We have spoken of the "law of tithes" in the production of food, giving the rule-of-thumb figure of 10 to 1. Thus ten pounds of grain or other feed produces one pound of meat. More accurate figures show that the following conversion ratios can be attained by modern meat production methods:

Meat Source	*Pounds of Feed to Produce One Pound of Meat*
Lamb	8.7
Beef	8.0
Pork	3.6
Turkey	3.5
Eggs	3.1
Chickens	2.3
Milk	1.0

An even more accurate accounting method measures the amount of *protein* that must be fed to produce one pound of animal protein:

Meat: A Luxury Food • 69

Meat Source	Pounds of Protein to Produce One Pound of Meat Protein
Lamb	12.5
Beef	10.0
Pork	7.1
Turkey	6.2
Chickens	4.6
Eggs	4.1
Milk	3.9

Milk seems to be the best bargain coming from the law of tithes. Notice, too, that in the production of beef protein from feed protein, the ratio is an exact tithe, or 10 percent!

OUR VITAL NEED FOR MEAT

It is possible, by careful selection, to get a balanced diet on plants alone. During World War II a Japanese botanist proved this by keeping himself and sixty men alive for sixteen months in hiding in the Philippine Islands after they were taken over by the Allies. He did this remarkable thing by locating no less than twenty-five edible plants amidst what seemed barren wasteland. But while some plants have this amino acid and that vitamin, meat contains *all* the aminos in good quantity. For this reason meat protein is rated as higher in "biological quality" than an equal amount of plant protein.

Far more humans suffer from a shortage of protein than from lack of calories themselves. It is the protein gap that plagues us, and it will continue to do so until more of our number have meat available to them in greater quantity. We like meat and crave it not just because it tastes good but because it *is* good. Fish, meat, and animal products rank at the top of the protein scale, as we saw in Chapter 4. Despite the law of tithes, then, meat is not so much a luxury as a nutritional necessity.

CHAPTER
6

The Agricultural Revolution

Some historians list three "giant steps" made by man toward the civilized world we know today. The first of these was speech. The third was writing. But between these giant steps in communication, so necessary to society, there came a second step of more vital importance. The second giant step was agriculture.

Perhaps 12,000 years ago man began to domesticate the animals he had previously hunted for food. This was a big step forward, for it assured him of a regular supply of meat. He also "harvested" wild grains and vegetables and fruits, timing his journeys if he was a nomad so that he would be on hand for a new crop. About the time of the domestication of animals, man began to domesticate the plants too. This agricultural revolution was the giant step that made it possible for billions instead of millions to live on earth.

We have mentioned the law of tithes in the food chain, requiring ten pounds of plant food to produce one pound of meat. When man learned to till the soil and reap the harvest he planted he made it possible to feed ten men where only one could have subsisted before. Agriculture, then, was of even more importance in its revolutionary effect than the previous advances in culture that had brought man fire and tools and weapons, for agriculture made it possible for a man to provide food for more than himself and his immediate family. Men freed from food-producing could turn to science and the building of governments.

Bread and other foods made with cereal grains sustain most of our population. Rice supports more than half the world's people, and wheat many of the others. Corn, another cereal grain, is the mainstay of Latin Americans, for "maize" was developed in the New World.

The cereal grains are only a few of the hundreds of thousands of "flowering plants" that convert sunlight, water, carbon dioxide and nutrients into food that man and the animals can eat. Trees are plants; so are the grasses in our lawns (and the weeds too). We can't eat trees or grass, but we do eat fruit from some trees, and we eat grass indirectly, by processing it through our livestock to produce meat.

As the Bible tells us, the plants necessarily came first (over 400 million years ago, in the case of land plants), because only plants can provide themselves with food from the basic resources. Grasses (and grazing animals) appeared within the past 50 million years. Like other animals, man is a predator, feeding on other living things. Fortunately for him, he is by nature omnivorous. However, communities of food gatherers rarely reach numbers of more than one or two hundred, and their kind of culture cannot support more than one or two people per square mile except in rare cases. Today we must depend on agriculture, the *cultivation* of plant life, for most of our food.

THE COMING OF FARMING

A nomadic existence does not permit a true agricultural society, although there are some nomads today who do carry along seeds on their wanderings and occasionally try for a crop after especially good rains. For real farming, a people must settle on the spot to tend the soil and the crops they plant, rather than only return periodically as in the older days of food-gathering.

We do not know to a fine degree of accuracy just when man learned to farm. This is because farming came long before writing; in fact, until farming gave man the leisure time needed he could not develop writing. Since writing was invented about 6,000 years ago, we *can* safely say farming came somewhat earlier than this.

Scientists who have done some shrewd detective work set the date for the coming of farming roughly 10,000 years before Christ. We know that by this time men had learned to hunt and fish with clubs, spears, hooks, and nets. Men had also learned, perhaps as early as 40,000 B.C., that the growth of some of the edible plants they fed on was seasonal. Still nomads, or wandering peoples, they may well have timed their travels to return at the proper season to areas where grasses or vegetables grew. It was inevitable that someone—a woman, most likely—noticed that this plant food grew from seeds scattered on the ground. The next step was intentionally to "plant" seeds close to camp; or perhaps the reverse was true, and camp was established close to where these primitive women farmers sowed their first seeds.

Archaeological findings seem to indicate that the earliest animal raisers were not yet planting their own food; however, they were harvesting wild plants. The remains of well-worn stone sickles and mortars in the Middle East prove this. It is believed that the sheep herders of Shanidar ground acorns and wild cereal grains on these mortars and stored meal or flour for future use, since fragments of crude baskets made from twigs were found.

Anthropologist Robert J. Braidwood of the University of Chicago has found carbonized or burned kernels of two kinds of wheat near the old stone ovens of a people who lived and tilled the soil in Jarmo, Iraq (not far from Shanidar), as long as 6700 B.C. These wheats differ very little from wheat grown in the area now, and interestingly the population of the area is also about the same as it was when Jarmo was a village—perhaps one of the first agricultural villages—supporting about 150 people. The time for the coming of agriculture seems pinned down between about 9000 B.C. and 6750 B.C.

Men advanced from being sheepherders and random pickers of fruits and plants to become producers of agricultural foods and tillers of the soil. As mentioned, in *Genesis* we read that God was more pleased with herdsman Abel's offerings of fat meat than he was with Cain's vegables. So distressed was Cain that he committed the first murder by killing his brother. In time, however, farmer and rancher learned to get along, and now both practices are often carried on by one man.

Farming did not sweep the world at once. It is believed by some scientists that it came first in China and the Near East, reached Greece and Italy about 5,000 years ago, was introduced in England only as late as the time of Julius Caesar's conquest of the Islands, and came to Scotland 500 years after that, or only 1,500 years ago! Today, there are still tribes in Australia that do not practice farming but live like Stone Age men. And some Eskimos may live entirely on fish and meat rather than tend farms.

One not readily obvious result of agriculture was the new availability of food for animals, and the primitive farmer first thinking of this application might have rejected the approach. Why feed crops to animals when he could not feed all his people on animals in the first place? But much of the cultivation of his fields, the "fodder" of cornstalks, for example, was of no nutritive value to man and made excellent animal feed. And since livestock were needed for draft power on the farm, and their manure was rich fertilizer, the followers of Cain and of Abel were inevitably drawn together instead of continuing their separate ways.

THE COOKING OF FOOD

There was an important discovery man made long before he took advantage of the cereals. That was fire and its application in cooking. Charles Lamb's "Essay on Roast Pig" surmises how the discovery of cooking meat came about in the accidental burning of a house in ancient China. Man must have discovered the joys of cooking grain cereals and other vegetables in a similar manner. Popped corn, a species in which the starch heats quickly and explodes, may have been the first edible corn. When heated, or "parched," wheat also pops open, shedding the hard husk. Parching was probably the first method of cooking wheat.

Parched corn, available in our country as a novelty, is still a standard food in parts of the Near East. Scots not long ago removed the "glumes" or husks from barley by setting fire to the unthreshed heads of the grain. And anthropologist Paul Mangelsdorf reports that Chippewa Indians still prepare wild rice by heating the unhusked kernels and then tramping on them in a hollow log to remove the hulls. Like corn, rice can be popped, and in India some villages even have a local "popper" who pops rice in a barrel of hot sand, collecting a portion of the rice as his fee.

Always seeking different tastes, man progressed to grinding the parched kernels of wheat or other grain and then soaking it in water to make meal. Great benefits have long been ascribed to cereals, as well to eggs and milk, as foods for the young. Gruel made from meal, and perhaps heated for taste as well as to warm the eater on a cold day, was a blessing to young and old—particularly those who might be toothless.

From gruel left standing after being prepared came another great development in cooking. This was breadmaking, which depends on the natural fermentation (infection with bacteria) of sugar in the cereal to make it rise, thus producing a light bread. Along with breadmaking came brewing, depending as it does on fermentation.

In ancient Rome and Greece, the diet of most people was bread, wheat or barley porridge, vegetables, fish, and spices. Describing the keeping properties of leavened bread, the Roman historian Pliny said: "Millet is especially used for making leaven. If dipped in unfermented wine and kneaded, it will keep a whole year . . ." He also described the brewing of beer from corn, with bread made from the foam as leaven, this making a "lighter kind of bread than other people's."

TILLERS OF THE SOIL

The farmer began with a few tools already on hand. Even in recent times women of the Paviotso tribe of North American Sierra Nevada Indians harvested wild grain from low grasses, beating it with a fan-shaped flail and gathering the seeds into a deep, conical basket carried with a strap over the shoulder. Because the remains of such baskets have been found in primitive diggings, it is probable that man many thousands of years ago had similar harvesting tools.

Early farming man had his stone sickles and mortars and even some crude metal tools. This took care of the harvesting and grinding. Most likely he first used his hands to dig the holes for planting seeds, and even to dig ditches for water when the idea of irrigation came to him. However, equipped with a sickle, spear, or club, he soon made makeshift shovels and picks for his digging tasks. Gradually a crude plow evolved, designed to be dragged laboriously through the ground by a man walking backward. Early plows were simply pieces of tree trunk and branch, which provided a fairly

Babylonian plow with seed-drill. From a Cassite cylinder-seal. Second millenium B.C. Illustration from *A History of Technology* (Singer et al, Oxford University Press)

efficient shape for churning up the soil. There are primitive farmers today who push their plows through the soil themselves, having improved only to the point that they can see where they are going. But early farmers in some lands hooked the plow to oxen, and their task then consisted of furnishing guidance instead of the motive power.

The first plows—most of them—had but one handle, since the plowman needed one hand free to hold the reins, or at least a whip or switch to control his ox or other draft animal. Recently when some farmers in underdeveloped lands were offered mechanized plows with two handles, they did not take readily to them, because by tradition they used the one-handle type.

In the early days stone, wood, or metal sickles or scythes sufficed for reaping the fruits of man's labors, but when he devoted all his time and energies to farming, improvements had to come in the harvesting department too. From a small, one-handed instrument, the scythe grew to a large, two-handed affair that cut a much wider swath and thus increased a man's productivity. Pliny describes an ingenious Roman "reaping machine" which was pushed, rather than pulled, by an ox. It used a rotary cutter mounted on the front to harvest ears of corn from the stalks. However, reaping was generally done by hand, as was threshing, until fairly recent times.

Gradually the old stone mortars gave way to larger and more powerful grinding mills, although there remained small handmills of the type issued to soldiers in Caesar's time so that they could prepare their own food in the field. Manpower, animal power, waterpower, and even windpower were used to drive the mills. There were similar presses developed to produce olive and other oils and also grape juice.

IMPROVING THE CROPS

When man depended on scattered clumps of vegetables and little patches of grain here and there, a given area of land could not keep many people alive, particularly when animals competed with man for much of this wild food. But when early farmers began to sow seeds in lines and rows that covered sizable fields, that same area began to produce huge amounts of food. Another factor that helped increase the yield of farm fields was the improvement of plant species through selection. There were many kinds of plants, and new species appeared from time to time through natural mixing. But man sought out those plants he thought best for his purposes and planted them. Thus, while he still had not learned how to prevent cross-pollination by the wind and insects, he did have an effect on the strains of plants that were grown.

Researchers digging in old village ruins in the New World have found the remains of tiny wild popcorn, ears only about half an inch long, and with about fifty tiny kernels. It was from this unpromising progenitor that farmers developed the corn we know today. Primitive farmers of course knew nothing of "plant genetics," back about 5000 B.C., when they were first using the tiny corn.

Not until Charles Darwin was there a formal concept of "natural selection"—of the survival of those plants and animals most suited to their environment. But early farmers scouting around for the most productive corns to plant were introducing a new kind of selection. Modern corn, with huge ears and up to 1,000 closely packed kernels per ear, cannot reseed itself and must be planted by man to keep going. Corn differs from wheat and some other grains that can still reseed themselves with no help from man. By the time Columbus reached the New World, farmers had improved corn by selection to the point where it produced ears about four inches long and perhaps 500 kernels instead of the 50 or so on natural maize. And Columbus, who brought some plants to America, had an excellent one to take back.

Once, an acre of land might have produced a few pounds of scrawny vegetables or wrinkled grain. Slowly men improved that yield until they harvested hundreds of pounds—and then tons—of food from a single acre. So productive did the land become that a relatively short time ago men had to hold back on planting because they just could not harvest wheat fast enough!

It is believed that irrigation was used even before man began to plant crops. Noting that wild grasses harvested for grain grew better near water, primitive collectors probably dammed streams and scratched shallow ditches to carry water to them. Water may also have been simply splashed from a stream or spring onto the ground around it, or even carried some distance in pots. With agriculture came even more need for irrigation, and by 1500 B.C. such devices as the Egyptian *shaduf,* or water lifter, were in general use. Similar contrivances were used in Babylonia, perhaps even as early as 2500 B.C.

Irrigation of a palm garden by shaduf in Egypt. The gardener has dipped his bucket into a pool surrounded by marsh plants, and the clay counterpoise has raised it to the level of the sloping funnel. Water will fill the mud basin at the foot of the tree. From a tomb at Thebes. C 1500 B.C. From *A History of Technology* (Singer et al, Oxford University Press)

Over the centuries man learned the importance of fertilizing his crops. In addition to air, water, and sunshine, plants require several nutrient chemicals for proper growth. Before the cultivation of fields, either nature had to replace these nutrients or man simply sought out more fertile areas for his food gathering. Now, as he tilled the soil and quickly depleted its nutrient chemicals, he learned that he had to replace them with manures, decaying plant matter, animal matter—or fish, as demonstrated by the

Indians of North America for the Pilgrims. Fertilization of a scientific nature was long in coming and has been practiced for a relatively short time in the over-all history of agriculture.

THE CEREALS

Of the 350,000 or so plant species, about 250,000 are of the flowering, seed-producing type. From this great variety man has selected little more than a dozen for the bulk of his food supply. These include rice, wheat, corn, white potatoes, sweet potatoes, sugar cane, sugar beets, cassava, beans, soybeans, peanuts, coconuts, and bananas. Of course there

Agricultural experts claim Ethiopia could be the granary of the Middle East and Africa if properly exploited. Here helpers set up devices for measuring the depth of the Awash River under a Government program helped by the U.N. Special Fund and FAO. FAO Photo.

are many others. It is estimated that about 3,000 have been used to some extent in man's history. Some of these we no longer use; some we have only recently begun to eat. The tomato is an example. For centuries it was known but considered poison because it belonged to the "deadly nightshade" family. When a man in America ate a tomato in public he was regarded at first as some kind of suicidal lunatic, then as a hero, and finally as the man who gave the country a very popular and nutritive food.

Of the several classes of plant foods, including cereals, vegetables, sugars, fruits, and nuts, the earliest to be cultivated were probably the grains. Why were the cereals so popular then and now? One reason is their durability. A sweet potato will keep for a little while, a peach for something less, but rice and wheat kernels can be stored for months and years. In fact, stories are told of seeds thousands of years old sprouting when planted. Because grain, or flour made from it, could be stockpiled against lean times, as Joseph did for the seven years of famine in Egypt, grains became the basis for the food supply of much of the world, particularly in areas of high population.

There are three major kinds of wheat, grouped according to the number of chromosomes they possess. *Einkorn* wheat has 7 chromosomes.

With advanced techniques, improved strains and heavy use of chemical fertilizers, Japanese farms (less than 2½ acres on the average) are among the world's most productive. With only 13.9 percent of its land cultivated, Japan has a normal annual yield of 12 million tons of rice. FAO Photo.

Emmer has 14 chromosomes, and the so-called *bread-wheat* group has 21 chromosomes. It is believed that emmer was the first wheat to be cultivated. By the Iron Age the bread-wheats were economically important.

Scientist Paul Mangelsdorf points out that wheat today is still the world's most widely cultivated plant and describes the "intimate relation between cereals and civilization." More than almost any other plant, cereal grains approach a complete diet, with carbohydrates, proteins, fats, minerals and vitamins. Wild barley has also been found in archaeological diggings. It is believed that oats and barley both were introduced into Europe along with wheat as weeds but were later developed as grains in their own right.

Ancient Asian civilizations relied on rice or wheat; the Greeks, Egyptians, and Romans used wheat and barley. In the new world corn was the mainstay. The Indians of Guatemala still live on a diet of about 85 percent corn and do fairly well on it. Rye is grown in some countries and substitutes for wheat. Rye bread is delicious and favored in Russia, Poland, Germany and the Scandinavian countries. Grains called sorghums and millets are also used by some peoples, perhaps a third of the world's population. In the United States we raise some sorghum and millet but feed it to our livestock.

VEGETABLES

Although the cereals are thought to have been cultivated first by primitive man, it is likely that he also farmed other plants. A diet of all wheat, all rice, or all corn quickly becomes unappetizing. It also lacks vital food elements. So man supplemented his diet with other plants, among them a class called *Legumes.* Peas, beans, and lentils, rich in protein, are legumes. Soybeans are another example of this kind of plant, now used much more than in the past. Chick peas are particularly high in protein, and the lima bean, which seems quite starchy, is one of the best all-round vegetable foods known. Since the legumes are often found as weeds in fields, they most likely would have invaded cultivated fields of grains and been discovered in that way if no other. They store well, and so would have been attractive crops.

Because vegetables are not as durable as kernels of grains and are less likely to have been preserved by carbonizing in ovens, it would not be

The Agriculture Revolution • 81

expected that records of their cultivation would be as well preserved. However, it is known that peas were on the diet of some early peoples as early as 4400 B.C. Lentils are known to have been in cultivation in Khafaje, Iraq, about 3000 B.C.

As long as five thousand years ago, peoples of North and South America cultivated peppers, beans, and squash along with their corn. For at least two thousand years the New World has had pumpkins, cocoa, peanuts, sunflowers, and sweet potatoes.

Four thousand years ago Old World farmers tended apples, apricots, bananas, cabbage, dates, cucumbers, grapes, olives, pears, peaches, tea, and watermelons. For at least two thousand years carrots, celery, asparagus, grapefruit, mustard, lettuce, lemons, oranges, plums, peas, and sugar cane have been cultivated. Onions, too, were cultivated in early farm fields, and ancient record tell us that workers on the Cheops pyramid were supplied with onions and garlic, as well as radishes, in their diet. Pliny writes of radishes "as large as a child's head," although when such giants are grown today they are generally so watery as to be useless as food.

In some South American countries and South Sea islands, the sweet potato or yam is the staple food. Some tropical peoples eat the starchy root plant, or *tuber,* called the cassava. We know the cassava as tapioca, from which we make pudding, but cassava eaters bake the vegetable into cakes, much as others do with wheat or corn.

White potatoes are another staple, although the Irish, who gave the plant its popular name, no longer depend on them so completely. Polynesians cultivate a root plant called taro, which is potatolike and eaten whole or made into a paste. Its green leaves are also eaten. Islanders eat lots of breadfruit, coconuts, bananas, and limes.

About sugar cane, used as a sweetener, we know little. It does not grow wild, and the first mention of it seems to be in Hindu mythology. Some historians believe it originated in New Guinea. The word saccharin derives from Sanskrit, incidentally. Greek and Roman writers called sugar cane "the grass which produced honey without the help of bees." The sugar from cane is identical with that from sugar beets, which were cultivated much later.

Very early in time travelers began to carry plants and seeds with them to introduce in new lands. Although some plants will still grow only in

Western Nigerian mothers, babies on their backs, crush cassava in the street. FAO Photo by C. Bavagnoli.

certain places, many transplants did take root and became important crops. Wheat in North America is one example; rice is another. Potatoes were brought to Ireland and became the basic crop—tragically it turned out, for when blight destroyed the potatoes millions of Irish starved.

THE "TREE CROPS"

Even apes and monkeys eat fruits, and early man must have favored this easy way to harvest food. However, the natural cultivation of fruit trees is a longer process. A crop could not be ready for picking for several years, whereas grains or vegetables produced in less than a year. However, apple halves are found in the remains of Late Neolithic German and Swiss lake dwellings. It is thought they were cut for drying. Another thing that makes it difficult to date the cultivation of fruits is that in the process their changes were not so dramatic as the development of selected grains.

In North America the acorn and buckeye nut were gathered and ground into meal. Acorns contain tannin, a bitter substance, and buckeye nuts are poisonous. So the Indians learned to leach these substances from the meal with hot water, after placing the meal in a depression in the sand. Trees were probably not cultivated for crops of this kind. Forests were close by, and there must have been little need to transplant or plant seeds, since the nuts were storable over long periods of time. The hazelnut is a good example. Popular today, it is still mostly wild.

BEVERAGES AND SEASONINGS

In milk and water man has two excellent drinks; in salt he has a popular flavoring for his foods. However, over the years he has added a number of beverages and dozens of seasonings to add variety and spice to his meals.

Coffee is said to have been discovered when an Arabian goatherd's animals were stimulated from eating the "fruit" from certain wild bushes. Soon thereafter, coffee became popular in the city of Mecca. In the fifteen centuries since then, it has become a major part of the food industry. Although it is not nutritious, coffee has been used as a food, as wine, as medicine, and as a beverage. Perhaps its most unusual use came came

Three stations and two substations of Ethiopia's Institute of Agricultural Research, FAO-directed, Government-sponsored, U.N. funded, are working to increase the yield of Ethiopia's agriculture, which represents 93 percent of its exports. Workers sort coffee beans at a clearing plant in Addis Ababa. FAO Photo by Y. Nagata.

Cleaning dry tea leaves in a factory in Kandy, Ceylon. FAO Photo by Woodbridge Williams.

when Brazilians, faced with a declining coffee market in the 1930s and 1940s, burned millions of bags of it as locomotive fuel!

More than sixty million 132-pound bags of coffee were used in a recent year, and worldwide the trade amounted to $2 billion. Scandinavians and Americans are the world's greatest coffee drinkers.

Tea is also a popular drink around the world, although its total production of about 2½ billion pounds a year is only one-third that of coffee by weight. Originating in Asia, tea remained almost exclusively a Chinese and Japanese drink until late in the eighteenth century. Then it became popular in Europe and has since spread to North America and elsewhere. The British are the champion tea drinkers, consuming it about as we do coffee.

Legend says that tea was accidentally discovered in 2737 B.C. by the Emperor Shen Nung, when some leaves fell by chance into a pot of boiling water. The fragrance captivated the emperor and he made it the national drink.

Columbus saw cocoa beans, from the cacao tree, when he came to America, but he regarded them as only a curiosity even though the natives had enjoyed them for centuries. Perhaps one reason was that it was customary to make a drink combining cocoa, corn, beans, spices and water! It was the explorer Cortez who finally introduced Europeans to cocoa, sweetened with sugar, as the delicious drink we enjoy today. Unlike coffee and tea, cocoa has appreciable food value.

Not until the eighteenth century was chocolate made from cocoa beans. Later milk was added to it to make milk chocolate, and today it would be hard to imagine a world without chocolate in its many forms. Today, as cocoa, cocoa butter, and chocolate, the cacao accounts for worldwide trade in excess of $500 million.

Columbus was looking for spices when he stumbled onto America. In ancient times great fortunes were built on the spice trade, which shows how much men are willing to pay to please their palates. The true spices include pepper, vanilla, cloves, cinnamon, nutmeg, ginger, cassia, mace, allspice, tumeric, and many other aromatic substances that come from tropical plants. We import more than $30 million worth into the United States each year.

Spices not only make our foods taste better but also are used to preserve some foods. There are other seasonings that are not true spices, among them the seeds of anise, celery, dill, and poppy. "Culinary herbs" include bay, chervil, parsley, mint, and sage. Finally there is a group of seasonings called "condiments," which includes mixed seasonings like catsup, curry powder, and mustard.

Like the frosting on the cake, these beverages and seasonings greatly enhance the pleasure we get from eating. A few cents' worth of salt a month makes a world of difference in the taste of meat, soups, and vegetables. And there are some people who can't seem to get started without a cup of coffee or some other beverage in the morning.

CHAPTER

7

Food—Our Largest Industry

When men lived as hunters and gatherers there were perhaps no more than five million people in the entire world. Today there are more than 3½ billion who must eat, and each year the world produces almost two billion tons of food. About 80 percent of this comes from farm crops, the remaining 20 percent from fish and meat products.

Such an abundance is not easy to provide. As long ago as 1800, Thomas Malthus, an English minister and economist, prophesied that the world would soon run out of food. The production of food is the world's number one priority. Even in the United States, where the work of one farmer can now produce enough food for more than forty people, farming is still our biggest business. It is no longer our only business, however, as it was before agriculture took the place of hunting and gathering.

The key to food plenty lies in treating the production of food as an industry that must be operated just as other industries are with regard to productivity, efficiency, economy, and distribution. Food production is too important now to be the concern only of the man with the hoe. It is a sad fact that in those countries where farming continues on a subsistence basis, using age-old techniques, there is far more want and hunger than in those countries where farming is an industry.

A locust swarm in Ethopia of the kind that has plagued mankind from ancient times, now well controlled under U.N. supervision. FAO Photo.

BIOLOGY IN FARMING

The improvement of agriculture has not been quick or easy. When man—having by that time taken over from woman as the farmer!—changed the nature of things in the plant world, he brought trouble on himself from the animal kingdom. While there had been a great variety of plants in an area, there was also great stability in the ecology of that area. That is, there was a variety of animal and insect life feeding on the various plants without nurturing overwhelming numbers of any one species. But when whole fields of grain, or peas, beans or potatoes stretched out invitingly before hungry creatures that thrived on those plants, nature was deprived of checks and balances and ran wild. The handful of pests that once preyed on scattered patches of wild wheat or vegetables multiplied incredibly until hordes of them appeared and wiped out man's crops, often in a single day. With huge crops came similarly huge clouds of locusts.

Writings from ancient times up to very recently were filled with tales of the suffering and hunger these pests left behind after they had ravaged the fields.

Man was grateful to insects for their help in some things. Bees, for instance, produced honey for their human keepers. Other insects joined the bees in pollinating fruits and other plants. Some insects ate other insects and thus got rid of crop pests. But man had to help in this police work too. For large food thieves like rabbits he could set traps or use weapons with some effectiveness. Insect pest control required the use of smoke and fire and finally of chemical treatment. Pesticides made it possible for man to grow large single crops and harvest most of them for himself instead of just providing free lunch for locusts, weevils, and grasshoppers.

Plants have other chemical needs too, and nutrients are high on the list of requirements for our crops. Nitrogen, sulfur, and phosphorus are naturally present in the soil, but nature did not plan on huge leveled, ploughed, and irrigated fields, with large crops draining the soil of its nutrients in short order. In early times various schemes were discovered or invented to take care of this problem. The first was simply to move on to new and fertile fields when an old one was depleted of nutritive elements. Another was "fire-cultivation" farming, the burning of trees and other vegetation to fertilize fields. While such burning is still practiced in some areas of the world, it is not practical on a large scale, for there is not that much land.

The "rotation" of crops was found to help; that is, planting one crop one year and another kind the next year or in two years. This took different chemicals from the soil instead of depleting the same ones and gave nature a chance to put back what man took away. Domesticated animals contributed manures to the soil, of course. But this was not enough to meet the scale of forced production that plants were being forced to meet. "Fallowing," or allowing a field to remain idle, became a practice. A farmer might have a third of his lands unplanted at any given time, simply allowing them to "rest up" for next year.

Supplemental fertilization with chemicals made it possible to farm a field every year. It also made it possible to produce more on it than only nature's fertilizers could produce. It would have been difficult centuries ago to convince farmers—who were the consumers of their own produce—to add artificial fertilizers to the soil. Today there are many consumers who protest chemical fertilization of land and demand a return to "organic" farming, manuring with animal wastes only.

Man had known for thousands of years that animal wastes helped his crops. The writings of Marco Polo indicate that the Chinese used fish for fertilizer, as the American Indians were doing when the first white men came to this continent. Not until about the middle of the nineteenth century, however, did German chemist Justus von Liebig conduct experiments with chemical fertilizers. He was convinced that soil lost its fertility simply because the minerals in it were exhausted. This seems obvious to us today, but it was an earth-shaking idea in Liebig's time. Experiments by French agriculturist Jean Boussingault had seemed to show that peas and beans took in nitrogen from the atmosphere, and unfortunately Liebig accepted this idea, maintaining that only sodium, potash, calcium, and phosphorus need be added. This shortcoming delayed the full benefit of chemical fertilizers until other men found that nitrogen, actually the most needed, was provided by bacteria growing about the roots of the plants.

Fortunately the chemical industry was developing at this time, and dependable sources of artificial fertilizers began to become available. During World War I the German chemist Fritz Haber learned how to produce nitrogen from the air. Although his primary goal was to produce explosives for the German military, Haber's discovery provided fertilizer for agriculture as a spin-off, and he was later awarded the Nobel Prize in chemistry for it.

The primary nutrients for agriculture are nitrogen, phosphorus, and potassium; "secondary" nutrients are calcium, magnesium, and sulfur. These six are called *macronutrients* since they are required in appreciable amounts. *Micronutrients,* of which only a few pounds per acre serve greatly to improve the crops, are boron, copper, manganese, chlorine, iron, molybdenum, and zinc. It is interesting to compare these plant nutrients with those required by man, as listed in the chapter on nutrition.

It was thought at first that adding chemicals simply made it possible for land to produce as efficiently as ever. As the science of fertilization developed, however, it was found that using more fertilizer and matching it to the crops greatly increased yields. Today about one-fourth of the food grown in the United States is credited to fertilization. So effective are fertilizers that conventional crops grown with large amounts of them have a tendency to "lodge," or fall over with the additional weight. Plant breeders have found it necessary to breed new plants that do not grow as tall.

The corn Columbus took back to Queen Isabella was a far cry from the pathetic-looking plant of 5000 B.C., and corn today is much different from that of A.D. 1492. Using the Mendelian theory of genetics and inheritance, breeders have developed hybrid corns, using the principle of *heterosis*. By making corn fertilize itself to isolate a pure strain, and then cross-breeding such strains to achieve "hybrid vigor," or extra growth, breeders have more than doubled the yield of corn per acre from about 25 bushels to the acre in 1916 to 60 and 70 bushels per acre today. The most recent development in corn is the breeding of strains that have a far higher content of lysine, an important amino acid in which corn is traditionally low.

Other grains have been hybridized, too, and today there is a "miracle wheat" that is a dwarf in comparison to older strains and yet produces far more per acre. There is "miracle rice" too. It is small and strong and does not "lodge" and thus lose its productivity. Work is now being done toward adding protein to enrich rice.

THE FARM "ENGINEERS"

Agriculture quickly made it possible to increase population density, as the 27-per-square-mile at Jarmo indicated. But the fact that the density in the area today is still only about that number is proof that the practice of basic agriculture itself does not guarantee support for large numbers of people. This abundance comes only with sophisticated agricultural techniques and improvements in crops, farming methods, and food processing and distribution.

Today one man sitting in comfort in a gasoline-powered combine can harvest enough wheat in one day to bake about a third of a million loaves of bread. This is enough calories to feed a third of a million people for one day! The first farmers did well to provide enough grain to feed themselves and their children, with the children probably helping out in the fields. One of the major reasons for this great difference in agricultural productivity is, of course, mechanization.

The poet Edwin Markham, inspired by Millet's painting entitled

A mature, bearded wheat variety and, *below,* superior strains of corn, have triggered a "green revolution" and given some a respite from food production worries. (Rockefeller Foundation Photos).

"The Angelus," wrote "The Man With the Hoe."

> Bowed by the weight of the centuries, he leans
> Upon his hoe and gazes on the ground,
> The emptiness of ages in his face,
> And on his back the burden of the world.

Later in the poem, Markham bitterly asks:

> O masters, lords and rulers in all lands,
> Is this the handiwork you give to God?

There are still men with hoes, of course, and even men who pull plows. But there have been great improvements in the hardware used in food production. The farm has been mechanized to such an extent that the farmer is now as much engineer as tiller of the soil.

The first plows were crude affairs, consisting of the basic digging stick or "share," an arm to attach it to the plowing animal, and a guiding handle. By about 1,000 B.C. the plowshare was made of iron in advanced agricultural societies. Several centuries later came the "coulter," a blade that ran ahead of the plowshare to help dig a deeper and straighter furrow. A thousand years later came the wooden "moldboard," a large vee-shaped extension of the plowshare that rolled back the soil like the wake of a boat, better aerating the soil and also turning up weeds. "Harrows" were used in Roman times, consisting of flat wooden frames with spikes driven into them. These were used for lightly turning the soil, for example to cover seeds just planted. In the Middle Ages there were rolling harrows, in which the flat frame was replaced by wheels fitted with spikes.

As late as the first half of the nineteenth century the ancient "cradle" was used in harvesting grain. But in 1831 young Cyrus McCormick, only 21 at the time, demonstrated his mechanical reaper in Virginia. Although still horsedrawn, the reaper harvested as much oats as five men. However, not until McCormick moved near to the wheat fields of the Midwest did his new idea catch on. In 1847 he set up shop in Chicago and within two years he was selling a thousand machines a year. Within a decade some 20,000 reapers a year were sold annually by McCormick and other manufacturers.

In Deaf Smith County, Texas, a farmer uses a four-row tractor and 14-foot John Deere wheat drill for seeding his winter wheat, while (*below*) another farmer not far to the south of him, in Mexico, is making do with a spike-tooth drag harrow home-made out of a railroad tie and some long spikes. U.S. Department of Agriculture.

The reaper wasn't the last word in farming for long. By 1880 it was superseded by the "combine," which did just that: combine the operations of reaping and threshing. The importance of such farm equipment lies in the fact that until it came along farmers could not plant much wheat. When ripe, the grain must be harvested in a very few days or it will fall to the ground and be wasted. Working with primitive equipment, even 80 percent of the work force in America (for that many were farmers as late as 1830!) could not farm all the good land available. But with reapers and combines, huge new acreages were opened up and food production began to increase, even with fewer and fewer farmers tilling the soil and reaping the harvest.

From the primitive basic plow came today's modern plow, cultivator, harrow, and rake, all pulled by a tractor rather than by animals or man. Some 12,000 years ago the farmers in Jarmo used their crude stone sickles to harvest wheat. There are still primitive Indian women who walk through wild wheat, sweeping grain from the stalks into large baskets tied to their sides. But there are also huge gasoline-powered combines that harvest and thresh 75 acres of wheat in a single day. There are still rice farmers who patiently set out plants by hand, walking barefoot in the muddy paddies. There are also those who fly airplanes and plant 400 acres of rice in a day. Machines level the ground, plough, harrow, rake, and cultivate it. Other machines pick and bale cotton, dig up and shell peanuts, and cut alfalfa and press it into pellets just the right bite-size for the cattle it will fatten.

Automatic sprinkling machines roll through fields, and some watering is even done *under* the ground. Huge dams store water for irrigation, and canals hundreds of miles long carry water to distant fields where there is insufficient rainfall for farming. Water is reclaimed from sewage for use in irrigation and helps open up lands previously uncultivated because of lack of water. We have even reached the point of producing rain and snow artificially by seeding the clouds with dry ice, silver iodide and other "nucleating" agents.

The productive farmers of today are not Markham's men with hoes but scientifically and technically trained experts. Their tools include the hoe and the plow, but also the airplane and the computer. Even spacecraft and sophisticated "remote sensing" techniques are being used in modern agriculture.

The glory of Egypt, the Aswan High Dam, built with the help of the Soviet Union. Finished, it will add half a billion dollars annually to the national economy, but galloping population growth can outspace its improved cropland output in a dozen years or so. WFP/ FAO Photo by P.A. Pittet.

ANIMAL HUSBANDRY

In the broad sense, agriculture includes the production of meat as well as plants for food. The raising of beef, pork, lamb and other meat animals has come as far from primitive times as has farming. Worldwide, in a recent year, there were 62 million tons of beef and pork produced, plus 325 million tons of cow's milk. Poultry accounted for more than 12 million tons of eggs and 7 million tons of meat. While man still provides himself with some wild game, most meat comes from pastures and feed lots.

Breeders have developed better meat-producing animals, better adapted to their environment and more resistant to pests and disease. *Bos primigenius,* the aurochs of old, would not recognize its progeny. Wild cattle produced little milk, but today's dairy cows yield milk and butterfat by the ton each year. With proper nutrition and medical care, animals are fattened much more rapidly than they were in the old times. More grain is fed to them than in years gone by, now that farmers are able to produce so much of it.

Perhaps remembering his tastes of thousands of years ago when he was primarily a hunter of game, man increases his consumption of meat and meat products as his income rises and he is able to afford more of this high-quality food.

Poultry is increasingly important as a source of meat protein, and new industries have sprung up for the purpose of mass-producing both chickens and turkeys on a highly efficient basis. Like fattening livestock in feed lots, factory-bred poultry are not allowed to move around much. Thus food is not wasted as energy or to build muscle, which will not be tasty.

In a recent year United States consumers averaged 167 pounds of meat apiece. However, even this high ration was far exceeded by several other countries. Argentina, for example, averaged 198 pounds per person, Uruguay 213 pounds, Australia 215 pounds, and New Zealand 233 pounds. New Zealand's meat consumption exceeded ours by about 40 percent.

The meat exporters are mainly Australia, New Zealand, Argentina, and, surprisingly, little Denmark, whose livestock production is truly amazing. England, the largest importer of meat in the world, gets about two-thirds of it from Denmark.

We have about doubled our consumption of meat in this country in the last thirty years, as it became economically possible for us to do so. We are the only country in the world able also to feed large quantities of grain to cattle, rather than keeping them on natural pasturage. As a result, a very high quality of meat is produced. Althrough the United States is the greatest producer of meat in the world, we also import another 1¼ billion pounds of it each year.

In a year the world produces enough meat for almost forty pounds per person on the average. Of course it does not go in equal quantities to all the world's people; those in the economically advanced countries eat a far larger share. In some countries, particularly India, the eating of meat is forbidden to many on religious grounds. Ironically, India has the world's largest cattle population, somewhat in excess of 235 million. The United States, with 104 million in 1964, is second, and Russia is in third place, with 87 million.

In most developing countries the raising of meat animals is hampered by animal diseases, as well as by a lack of knowledge or modern highly productive methods. Another factor is the preservation of meat. In advanced countries up-to-date slaughtering, preservation, and distribution practices guarantee that meat will stay fresh from slaughterhouse to supermarket, and then in home freezer or refrigerator until eaten. Most people in the developing lands do not have these modern conveniences, and their meat must be eaten very soon after it is killed. Africa's tsetse fly is a great menace to livestock herds, and, tragically, most children never get milk after they are weaned, because cow's milk is infected.

North America, Europe, Australia and New Zealand, with only about 20 percent of the world's population, produce 55 percent of the world's milk. The developing countries, representing some 60 percent of the population, produce only 20 percent. The milk and meat situations understandably are about the same, and for the same basic variables of economics, disease, and dairying methods.

Japan faces special problems. It is a developed country, and as its people become economically able to buy meat they acquire a taste for more and more. However, agricultural land is in short supply, and far fewer livestock can be supported per human in Japan than in the United States, Europe, Australia, or Argentina. Nevertheless, the Japanese are adopting modern methods of animal husbandry, and their production of meat, and particularly milk, is growing rapidly. Japan makes up its protein diet largely with a great per capita consumption of fish, about seventy pounds per person each year, compared with only ten pounds in the United States—which is the amount of *meat* the Japanese get, coincidentally!

HARVESTING THE SEA

Fishing is an ancient art that has been changed by science into a profession. Like farming and cattle-raising, it has been made into an industry by the developed countries. As a result, fantastic increases have been made in the sea harvest, particularly in the last two decades. About sixty-five million *tons* of fish were taken in a recent year, about half the weight of meat produced in a like period of time. However, much of the fish catch, as we have noted, is converted into fish meal for feeding animals for meat production. About 10 percent of the fish is taken from fresh water.

Southern waters began only in the 1950s to account for a major share of world fish production. Until then only about 2 percent came from below the Equator. Now the percentage has jumped dramatically to about 35 percent, largely because of the efforts of Peru and Chile.

On a worldwide basis, fish is not so important a food anywhere else as in Japan. We Americans have eaten an annual individual average of only about ten pounds of fish a year for many decades. But fish does supply about 20 percent of total protein needs around the world, and if we were suddenly deprived of the sea catch there would be a tragedy at the dinner table for many people.

Frozen tuna at the Tokyo Wholesale Fish Market. The fish were caught in the Indian Ocean between Madagascar and Ceylon. FAO Photo.

There was a time when it was thought that the sea could never run out of fish, no matter how large a catch fishermen hauled into their boats. Estimates are more realistic now, but there is a wide range, nevertheless. Some authorities feel that we cannot greatly increase present quantities; however, others predict an eventual fiftyfold increase in fish caught, working on the basis of how much plankton there is in the sea, and what fraction of that ends up as flesh in fish of a size and kind useful to the human diet. Interestingly, much of the fish caught goes to feed not man but animals. Chickens, hogs, and even cattle are fed on protein-rich fishmeal.

Even catching fifty pounds of fish for every pound now caught would not result in quite the blessing to food supplies it would seem. While fish take care of 20 percent of the animal protein needs in our diet, those needs represent only 10 percent of our total diet. Fish, then, are only 2 percent of all our food, and a fiftyfold increase in fish caught would just match the total amount of food consumed today. It would seem that at best our oceans will help us feed about twice the population we now have.

Aircraft, radar, sonar, and other sophisticated equipment make fishing far different from the old days of sailing ships. While most fish is still taken with hook or net, it is now taken faster and in hundredfold quantities. Modern electronically equipped, diesel-powered trawlers catch thousands of pounds of fish in a single hour, fish often spotted by electronic devices that probe far beneath the sea. Electrical lures, as well as air bubblers, are sometimes used to guide fish into the nets.

Contrast this with fishing in many developing countries where methods are the same as they were a thousand or more years ago. Oars or sails propel the boats, and the fishermen may spend most of their time going to the fishing waters and returning with a meager catch. The rowboat or sailboat fisherman averages about one ton of fish a year. Obviously these few pounds a day cannot amount to a large share of the world's catch. For example, most commercial fishermen average one hundred tons or more a year per man.

Although European fishermen have for four centuries traveled long distances to fish off the Grand Banks off Newfoundland or the Continental Shelf off Iceland, Greenland, and Norway, their range was limited by sailing speed, plus the fact that ice was the only way to preserve the catch. Today fast fishing craft and mechanical refrigeration permit longer trips and larger catches. Fishing is still an exciting and dangerous job in many instances, however, and it is becoming difficult to recruit fishermen for such long stays away from home.

Freezer-trawlers catch fish, filet them, and freeze them immediately. More than twenty countries have this kind of equipment, and the Russian catcher fleet includes more than 100 huge 3,000-ton craft, vessels far larger than anything we operate. Factory ships may be as large as 20,000 tons. The Japanese, too, have sophisticated fishing fleets that not only catch fish but freeze, cure, can, or process for fishmeal and oil right on the fishing banks. It is profitable for them even to fish in Atlantic waters, thousands of miles from home.

THE PRESERVATION OF FOOD

If plant crops grew all the time, or if meat animals could be killed for eating at any time, there would be less need for the storage of food. Since crops are largely seasonal, however, and animals are generally too large to consume at one or a few meals, man has for thousands of years stored part of the food he produces. In some developing countries storage facilities remain as primitive as those of centuries ago, and much food is wasted, lost to insects or animals, or spoiled by microorganisms. It is the proper storage of foods that has made civilized life possible. As a United states Department of Agriculture publication says, "If we could not preserve food in some stable form, people would forever be forced to live right where the food is produced, and there would be no agricultural trade."

Even in ancient times people stored certain foods for fairly long periods of time. They learned preservation processes mostly through chance and observation. The simplest method of preserving foods is to dry them in the sun, and sun-drying of many foods has been practiced by man for thousands of years. Drying preserves food because the moisture content of the food is reduced to such a low level that it will no longer support microbial life.

Grains are naturally protected. Vegetables—notably peas and beans—can be dried and stored. At a later time, when water is added, they regain their original size and consistency and can be cooked for eating. However, since they will now support microbial life—which has remained in them, dormant, during storage—they must be consumed within a short time.

Milk can be dried to powder by evaporating all the water. In this form it can be stored for long periods. It is also easier to transport, since most of the weight is taken away. Added water reconstitutes the powder into at least a semblance of the taste of fresh milk. In a single year of the Food for Peace program the United States shipped about 750 million pounds of dry milk to eighty countries. Japan imports great quantities of dry milk and attributes the increase in height and weight of its children to milk in school lunch programs.

Fruits and meat are also sun-dried, sometimes sliced to speed the process by exposing more surface to the sun's heat. Drying is only protection against spoilage, of course, and does not guard against infestation by weevils and other insects that feed on such food.

Perhaps thousands of years after he learned the secret of sun-drying—and still without knowing why such methods worked—man chanced on other methods of preserving foods. The smoking of meat and fish is an example. Since these foods would often be left near the campfire, where smoke would reach them, it is easy to imagine how such a preservation method was discovered. It is chemicals in the smoke that protect food from bacteria. Salt is another chemical preservative, and man may have learned its effectiveness from living and fishing near tidal basins that accidentally salted his fish. Later he salted meat too, just as effectively.

For centuries fishermen preserved their catches by salting, drying, smoking, fermenting or pickling. Today there are five main methods of using fish: cured in a variety of ways, canned, frozen, converted to fish meal or oil, or fresh. About a third of the world's fish catch is cured, 10 percent is canned, 20 percent is frozen, and 30 percent is converted to fishmeal. Thus only about 7 percent is used fresh.

Cold, as well as lack of moisture, stops the action of microbes in food. Early man learned that his food was preserved for him when it was frozen. A classic example is the thawing of wooly mammoths found frozen in the ice in Siberia an estimated 50,000 years after their deaths. When the meat thawed out, men could eat the preserved flesh! Eskimos and others living in frigid climates made such discoveries in the natural course of events. Later, men learned to saw blocks of ice from frozen lakes and use them for refrigeration. Cellars dug into the ground were to be useful for "cold boxes," as were wells and springs, which still serve for chilling many foods, including picnic watermelons.

Heat is another preservative. When food is cooked, the microorgan-

An early tourist's-eye view of American Indians smoking meat for preservation. Kean Archives Photo, Phila.

isms in it are not merely put to sleep but effectively killed. Ancient man discovered that cooking his meat and plants made it possible to store them for short periods.

"If you can't beat 'em, join 'em" is an old bit of advice that sometimes works to man's advantage. Man has learned to adopt this tactic with some of the microorganisms that attack his food. Probably from such a simple occurence as the fermentation of gruel left standing long enough came the arts of brewing, wine-making, and breadmaking with natural yeasts, and such fermented products as sauerkraut, pickles, and cheeses. In these cases the bacteria are allowed to consume part of the food, in the process protecting it from further spoilage and making it tastier.

All these preservation methods are ancient history, of course, but modern man has carried them far beyond their simple beginnings. Mechanical refrigeration, invented in 1834, has taken the place of ice, snow, and the pasture spring. Quick-freezing and freeze-drying, sometimes combined with vacuum-packing, make possible the preservation of foods for years if necessary. Pasteurization—the killing of bacteria by heating— and then canning or sealing up the protected food has become an effective process. Some foods accidentally kept in this way for more than a hundred years have been found to be still fit to eat.

Man has learned to use a great many chemical preservatives and even to apply nuclear radiation to foods to render them sterile. Processing and packaging techniques in combination with this method make it possible to preserve a great variety of products fairly cheaply. While we may frown at the long list of "additives" in our processed food, pining for the good old days when everything was natural and just like it was picked, a visit to countries forced to use the techniques of the good old days might quickly change our minds.

After long processes of research and convincing the authorities that "fish concentrates" are safe and healthful, the fishing industry now can grind whole fish and make a rich protein flour suitable for soups, bread, and other uses. While this product has not yet been widely accepted, millions of tons of fish are turned into easily stored fishmeal each year and used to fatten meat animals and poultry.

FROM FARM TO CONSUMER

Today, food processing is a multibillion-dollar business in the United States and many other countries. Few of us grow our own foods, and many of us have never drunk milk as it comes from the cow or eaten vegetables fresh from the fields. While these are pleasant ways to eat, our farmers, teamed with processing plants and supermarkets, make available to us a variety of foods our ancestors would not have believed possible. In our country such food handling is so efficient that we spend only about 18 percent of our budget on food, compared with some countries that spend half of their income or more on eating. Of course there are still some primitive people who literally spend their lives raising food.

Primitive men must have dried meats and fruits and taken them on their long treks, and the exchange of such items of food as citrus fruits is a matter of historical record. The spice trade and tea trades produced enormous changes in the course of history. But in the developed countries today as much as 90 percent of the food produced is marketed hundreds and even thousands of miles from the place where it was grown.

Foods, then, are preserved not only to be eaten at other times but at other places too. Often the "raw material" itself will travel a long way

Atlantic red hake and finished fish protein concentrate product. Six pounds of fish will produce one pound of the concentrate. Bureau of Commercial Fisheries Photo.

from farm to factory. Then, after being handled on a production line somewhat like a manufactured article—for many foods are indeed processed, or manufactured—the product is sent even farther for sale. This kind of trade requires good "farm-to-market roads"—shipping facilities that include not only railways, highways, and sea lanes but air freight also. Increasing amounts of food are being shipped by air. Fresh and perishable fruits are airborne, of course, as well as delicacies and staples like French bread, which is baked of soft flour and not good for many hours.

There was a time when families everywhere raised their own food, and there are still lands where most people engage in farming. Here, where only one man in forty is needed to produce food, and in many other parts of the world, most people now must buy it. We Americans generally do our marketing in supermarkets, where many thousands of attractively packaged products are available at reasonable prices.

The supermarket is a relatively new concept in food distribution. Beginning in the 1950s in the United States, the idea grew until now about half the food purchased in our country comes from these establishments. The reasons for their success are economic. A large store can offer a great variety of good food products at low prices compared to those of a small corner grocery of the kind that dotted the country not many decades ago. Many such convenience stores are still with us, of course, but more and more of our purchases are made in the supermarket. The same thing is true in Europe and in Australia, and there are supermarkets in some large cities in most countries of the world.

However, most people in the undeveloped countries still must buy—if they buy at all—from small stores, or from peddlers on the street corner or along the road. Colorful and nostalgic? Yes, but perhaps not as pleasant as it seems. For the peddler's wares may be poor in quality, or even spoiled. He will have little variety and the price must be haggled over. There will be no preservatives, no packaging, no frozen foods—just food as it came out of the field or from the slaughterhouse. Plus some bugs and flies, and maybe the danger of dysentery from eating it.

CHAPTER

8

The Problems of Pollution

Man began to contaminate the environment when he first began to breathe. Until relatively recent times this contamination—or pollution, to give its more honest name—has seldom been a widespread threat to our well-being. It is true that when Cabrillo first came to what is now the Los Angeles area, he found a layer of smoke from Indians' fires and the place was even then named "Bay of Smokes." London's reputation as a smoky, dirty city is historic, and today breathing there is actually at its best in many centuries. Generally, however, pollution in all its many forms is a growing danger and one that must soon be faced head on if we are to prevent the destruction of much that we find good in the world.

PESTICIDES

Today there are concerted efforts being made to abolish some pesticides. Some well-meaning but misguided people advocate wiping out all pesticides and returning to "organic agriculture," using only natural fertilizers and no chemical pest killers. Certainly if it were possible to feed the world without using poisons it would be not only ridiculous and uneconomical but criminal to continue to use them. For pesticides *are* deadly poisons that can—and occasionally do—kill people as well as pests. However, automobiles kill hundreds of times more people than do pesticides. Even aspirin kills more, and so does the antibiotic penicillin. We do not stop producing and driving automobiles however, because they are useful, sometimes vital, to our civilization. So are aspirin and other drugs. The same situation is true with respect to pesticides.

It has been a long time since man began to use pesticides of one kind or another. Greek writers long before the time of Christ described the use of chemicals for killing insects that preyed on crops. Such defensive actions were necessitated when man stopped depending on whatever meat and crops nature provided, wherever she provided them. Large fields planted to one species made an ideal lunch counter for insects or animals. The pests grew in numbers until they threatened to wipe out man's food supply, and naturally man fought back—with pest killers. He is still fighting today, and if we were suddenly to stop using pesticides there would be global famine from which the world as we know it would not recover.

It is charged, and quite accurately, that man is adding many tons of poisons to the environment each year with pesticides. It is also charged that some of these poisons are collecting in the tissues of plants and animals. This too is true. We have DDT in our own bodies, as do the lower animals and plants. There is DDT in our water, and residues of it are in food we eat and milk we drink.

Some critics charge that certain species of birds are being killed off by DDT; that the pesticide causes liver ailments and also thins the eggshells (although oddly, one species' shell—that of the Bengalese finch—seems to be thickened by DDT). Others claim that DDT is adversely affecting the photosynthetic process in the oceans.

Now, we should not tolerate a condition that in fact poses a threat to our lives or to our health. The Food and Drug Administration has monitored the effects of DDT for the more than twenty-seven years of its use. A long and detailed series of tests indicated that the chemical was safe as a pesticide. DDT was first used to control an epidemic of typhus in Italy during World War II. Deaths have occurred from DDT, in a factory producing the chemical in quantity, and to people using it to commit suicide. However, DDT has been eaten by mistake as flour for bread or pancakes without fatal results, although some of the eaters were very sick for a long time. And scientists and test subjects have taken large amounts of

DDT—a teaspoonful at a time, for instance—with no apparent harmful effects. The laboratory experiments that were claimed to show DDT harming algae growth required a concentration of the pesticide several hundred times the amount that could ever occur naturally in the ocean. And it has been pointed out that huge amounts of even so "safe" a chemical as salt can kill—and have done so—when improperly used.

Over the years an estimated 300 million lives have been saved through the control of malaria, typhus, yellow fever, and more than 20 other diseases with DDT. However, we are primarily concerned in this book with food, and it should be noted that DDT has also helped provide ad-

An FAO Freedom from Hunger Campaign sponsored by German Evangelical Churches and collaborating with a Government land development project proves that Liberia's swamps, cleared and properly irrigated, can grow improved strains of rice. Here the grain is hand-sprayed with an insecticide. FAO Photo by G. Tortoli.

ditional food, meat, and milk by controlling agricultural pests.

DDT is "persistent," which is one reason for belief that it is a menace and should be banned. Of course in pesticides persistence is a desirable quality making continuing control possible without the need of frequent applications of more dangerous chemicals. Nevertheless, it is not the persistence and accumulation in our bodies that is of primary importance, but what effect such accumulation has. This we cannot yet know.

Plants and animals do retain some DDT from what they eat, and at each step of the chain there may be higher and higher concentrations of the chemical. We also accumulate arsenic in our bodies, plus lead, zinc, and other elements.

DDT is being banned in some states, and pressure continues for its complete ban worldwide. But the World Health Organization, which has used it for decades to save lives, pleads that such a ban will leave them

Dead game at a water hole in Botswana. An even greater menace than poachers and uncontrolled hunters is the indiscriminate use of insecticides. FAO Photo by T. Riney.

without a safe and effective weapon. Although complete banning of DDT is probably undesirable, agency control by professionals is needed.

We cannot say that all is well with the use of pesticides. Much improvement must yet be made before we can say we have set our environment in proper order. As a California ecologist has charged, sufficient consideration may not be given to all aspects of poisons in the environment in developing new pesticides. Some farmers tend to rely on pesticide "overkill" and to spray by calendar rather than by the number of bugs in the field. This practice is wasteful and results in higher prices for the consumer. More importantly, it adds to the poisons needlessly contaminating our environment. Irrigation water, rain, and wind spread the pesticide around where it is not needed and often not wanted.

To this charge, some agriculturists reply that it is good insurance to use plenty of pesticides so there won't be any pests. Why wait until the bugs are ruining the crop and it is too late? they say. We can't wait until the house is on fire to have an appointment with our insurance man!

While there may be truth in such statements, it is shortsighted to lean too heavily on them as guidelines. "Overkill" can cause the destruction of insects actually beneficial to crops and to man generally. It can result in the development of insects resistant to the pesticides. In California the overuse of DDT is said to have caused the evolution of new insect strains so hardy that it has been necessary to change to more potent chemicals. As a result, bees have been incidentally and accidentally killed. Many beekeepers are out of business.

The improper use of pesticides has caused trouble also in the cotton fields of California, where the lygus bug and the cotton bollworm are the "key" pests. Perhaps a hundred other insects attack cotton, but none of them are serious threats, and there are also many beneficial insects in the fields. Some of these prey on the lygus bug and the bollworm. The indiscriminate killing of all insects with powerful and deadly chemicals can result later in invasion by the pests without any natural control at all, so that the farmer must spray again and again. This will be an increasing problem where DDT has been replaced with chemicals that are not persistent.

There is another pesticide problem in apple orchards of the state of Washington. Here, where apple rust mites prey on the crops, the tendency of orchardists is to use powerful, "broad-based" pest killers. This practice wipes out not only the rust mite but also the other mites that prey on it and help to control a third mite. The proper solution is to develop specific pesticides that kill only certain species or groups of species.

There are other ways of controlling pests. Encouraging work is being done in finding biological ways to eliminate a number of them. One good example is the case of the screw-worm fly, a pest that invades hot, humid climates and causes cattle infections. The U.S. Department of Agriculture over the years has developed a clever way to eradicate these pests. After breeding millions of screwworm flies in laboratories and sterilizing them by nuclear irradiation, USDA scientists introduce these nonproducing flies into the infested areas. Mating with natural flies, the sterilized flies produce no young, and very quickly the pests are completely eliminated. Similar work has been done with the melon fly and more recently with the pink bollworm. Here the "birth control" method is an excellent one for insects because it introduces no poison into the environment, and the flies themselves are no radiation hazard.

Even more subtle are some methods of using biological control in the form of other insect life. In the late 1800s, for example, the U.S. Department of Agriculture imported the vedalia beetle from abroad to control a kind of scale that was harming citrus crops in California. Sad to relate, the indiscriminate use of pesticides has killed such helpful insects.

Pesticides are polluting our environment, without a doubt. But to stop using chemicals immediately could cause chaos in agriculture. There must be much more study of the broad and long-range ecological effects of pest controls, plus diligent and forceful efforts toward using only the safest and most effective controls.

An even worse menace to our food supply are the industrial wastes that are dumped into our water supply and spewed into the air. Unlike pesticides, this form of pollution is no new outrage against nature. Through mining, man began to devastate the American countryside centuries ago. Perhaps it is impossible to mine without gashing the heart out of the land so used, but mines have done far more than scar the earth. Their smokestacks belch millions of tons of sulfur dioxide and other contaminants into the air—fumes that in some areas have denuded the trees and stripped all vegetation for miles around, particularly in the downwind direction. Pollution continues its dirty work many miles from the scene of the original source. Mines also drain poisons into lakes and

Despite conversion of poisonous smelter fumes to useful acids back in 1917, 100 square miles of land around the Tennessee Copper Basin (Ducktown) continued to erode for many years. This picture was taken in 1943, when the ecology was completely destroyed. Today the vegetation is beginning very slowly to come back. U.S. Department of Agriculture Photo.

rivers, killing the life in them. Even mines long since closed down continue to pollute the soil and water in this manner.

Crops suffer from mine smoke, and it is the practice in some places to reimburse the farmers for such losses. This, however, does not bring back the lost crops. Huge slag piles contribute choking dust when the wind springs up. Arsenic pumped out of mines and industrial plants poses a double hazard to humans and to animals—directly at first, and again when the living creatures feed on arsenic-poisoned vegetation.

Mines are not the only industrial offenders in the matter of pollution, of course. Industrial plants of many kinds distribute lead, mercury, fluorides, molybdenum, and other poisons to air, water, and countryside. The agriculture of Southern California, long an envied model for much of the country, has suffered heavily with the heavy industrialization of Los Angeles and the surrounding area. Flower-growing and farming businesses have suffered from ruinous blights since 1942.

THE SMOG MAKERS

Smog, the product of industrial pollution and the exhaust of automobile and truck engines, has been found to be damaging plant life in twenty-three states of our country and in the District of Columbia. This is not merely token or nuisance damage, either, for crop losses in Southern California alone have been estimated at $10 million a year.

Ozone, one constituent of the "photochemical smog" caused by sunlight shining on the dirty mass of smoky air, is a principal cause of blight in plants. Lead from gasoline, fluorides, nitrates, and sulfur dioxide are other noxious compounds. In both California and Florida, which are the leading citrus producing states, orchards have been heavily cut back in production because of smog losses. Lettuce and other leafy vegetables have been hard hit. So have beans and beets, celery, onions, turnips, radishes, potatoes and tomatoes—the vegetables we depend on for our food.

Besides crops, flowers, plants, and trees are being damaged. So bad is the atmosphere in New York City that City Hall plants must be taken periodically to a greenhouse to be revived. Elsewhere in the city plane trees and lindens suffer and die. Even in urban areas far from the downtown centers, evergreens, walnuts, elms, birches, maples, sycamores, ash and many other trees cannot escape the poisons in the air. The Ponderosa pine in Southern California suffers from "X disease," thought to be caused by pollution. And the eastern pine has not escaped either; blight strikes the same kind of trees in Tennessee.

We cannot put all the blame for air pollution on industry, much as we might want to. For automobiles are responsible for a major share—in some areas the overwhelming share—of smog. In this country, which is extremely dependent on automobiles, the internal combustion engine injects eighty million tons of pollutants into the air from exhausts and leaks elsewhere in the power system.

"Solid waste" is another of our pollution problems. Each American, on the average, contributes about 1,500 pounds per year of paper, garbage, trash, and other solid waste to be somehow disposed of. We also are each responsible yearly for about 750 pounds of pollutants added to the air. While aerial waste may not be so obviously littering the world we live in, it is even more dangerous than solid waste, because it endangers our own lives directly and that of our food supply.

A recent article on smog stated a frightening truth: "Sometimes it rains acid." This is what stings our eyes, causes respiratory ills, and disintegrates synthetic fibers, including women's nylons. "Killer fogs" composed of such deadly acids descended on Belgium's Meuse Valley in 1930; on the town of Donora, Pennsylvania, in 1948; and on London on several occasions, during one of which thousands of deaths were attributed in part to the choking smog.

As if these here-and-now terrors weren't enough, there are serious warnings that man, dumping 200 millions of tons of pollutants into the air in the United States alone in a single year, is raising the level of carbon dioxide in the air. Some scientists claim that as a result the temperature of the air is measurably higher than it was fifty years ago. Continuation of this warming trend could have serious effects on plant life, among other things. However, growing evidence indicates that dust accumulations are having just the opposite effect, cutting out sunlight and lowering temperatures in a perpetual twilight that is at least equally unfriendly to life.

DIRTY WATER

An insidious feature of air pollution is that after a time we become accustomed even to smog and almost think of it as "natural." The pollution of our streams is more obvious, and the evidence of desecration is disgustingly visible, but even the outwardly filthy appearance of some of our rivers, lakes, and even oceans does not hint at the extent of the pollution that has taken place. Samples of Ohio River water were recently scooped up near the city of Cincinnati, which draws its water from that river, and puts it back much the worse for wear. In the water, not surprisingly, were bacteria and viruses from sewage. There were also the following *organic* chemicals in the water: cyanide, phenols, and a variety of pesticides including DDT, Dieldrin, endrin, heptachlor epoxide, and toxaphene. The radioactive substances Radium 226 and Strontium 90 were also found. And this was only the beginning. The *inorganic* chemicals present read like a polluter's dictionary:

Ammonia	Iron
Arsenic	Lead
Barium	Manganese
Boron	Nitrates
Cadmium	Nitrates
Chloride	Phosphorus
Chromium	Selenium
Copper	Silver
Fluoride	Sulfate
Zinc	

The Cuyahoga River, near Cleveland, actually burst into flames, almost destroying two railroad bridges. In many cases this is water we must drink and use for cooking and other purposes—water we must use for irrigating our crops. Most of the water we drink is processed to remove dangerous organic pollutants, but little, if any, treatment is applied for metallic additives. And fish and other wildlife which we may later eat are completely unprotected. Millions of fish have been killed by pollution in streams, lakes, and the oceans. One killer we don't generally consider dangerous is hot water. Many industrial plants require water only for cooling purposes, a seemingly harmless use. But fish cannot tolerate temperatures much different from those they are accustomed to, and thermal pollution kills off wildlife in some waters. Temperature increases may be critical to spawning grounds.

There is a strange-sounding word that is increasingly often applied to our lakes. This word is *eutrophication,* which means the overenrichment of a body of water with nutrients. Eutrophication occurs naturally over long periods of time, stimulating excessive growth of algae and other water plants. But man has added his nickle's worth with sewage and other effluents, including phosphates from washday detergents, and for some lakes it has been too much. Fish are dying, or have already died long before their time, because the BOD (biological oxygen demand) of the organic decomposition process uses up all the free oxygen in water. And with them dies a part of our food supply and our pure water. The wild growth of plant

An Illinois state biologist measures victims of a massive fishkill in this picture taken by the Federal Water Quality Administration. Environmental Protection Agency Photo.

(*Below:*) Rome's "Father Tiber," one of the most important rivers of antiquity, is now choked with chemical and waste discharges, including oil, resulting in the killing of normal water-cleaning organisms and the death of fish. FAO Photo by P. Greene.

life is turning some waterways into weird jungles unfit for much other marine life.

Estuaries and the coastal waters of the oceans themselves are being dangerously polluted with sewage and industrial wastes. The oyster harvest in the United States is much reduced, because pollution has either killed off the shellfish or made them too dangerous to eat.

There is another kind of pollution often in the news now: the "oil spill." As early as the 1920s concerned conservationists pointed out that the oil industry made it a practice to dump crude oil residues, appropriately called "slop," at sea. Being lighter than water, oil floats, of course, and finds its way to shore to litter the beaches, often killing thousands of sea birds in its progress. Today the situation is made worse because of the ever-increasing shipment of oil by boat, and the practice of pumping oil from wells hundreds of feet below the sea. Offshore wells already make up about a sixteenth of world oil production and it is estimated that within a decade their number will increase by more than a half. One writer has expressed the opinion that through accidents and carelessness about one million tons of oil is spilled into the oceans each year.

Since some of the constituents of oil are toxic in high enough concentrations, and even carcinogenic, or cancer-inducing, oil spills may pose a danger beyond the outright killing of sea life by drenching it in oil. Fish could take in so much oil over a period of time that they might become contaminated as a food supply.

Most oil spills are accidental, and if we continue to drill under the sea for oil we may expect more accidents, since it is difficult to seal off a leaking well once it gets out of control. However, most water pollution is no accident. It happens simply because water has generally been the handiest place to dump something we want to get rid of!

Our sawmills dump waste into rivers and coastal waters to create a foul mess that stinks up the air for miles. Slaughterhouses dump everything imaginable into the water, We have mentioned mines, but chemical plants and metal industries contribute too. Even the farmers who produce our food add to the pollution by washing out excess pesticides and fertilizers in irrigation water. But, as in the case of our automobiles, we, the citizens of the country, must take the blame for sewage, the largest single source of pollution.

There was a time when there were so few people on earth that with reasonable care sewage was no big problem. Now there are so many of us that the waters of earth, once thought bottomless pits for all our garbage, are beginning to sicken and in some cases even to die.

Although we know that air, water, and carbon are used over and over in the food cycle, it is not obvious that we are breathing the same molecules of oxygen over and over again. It is easy, however, to see in many of our waterways that water is our most-used commodity. Some rivers serve cities whose water has been used a dozen times upstream before reaching them. Given space enough and time, Nature is a great purifier, and she used to clean up our messes without much complaint. But that time is gone for most developed and densely populated areas.

While we necessarily treat our water before we use it, we are not as careful when we dispose of it. There are, in fact, 1,400 communities in the United States that simply dump raw sewage, untreated, into the water! And a major number of the other communities give only partial treatment, ranging from a token filtering to removal of about two-thirds of the pollutants.

DIRTY WORLD

We are faced with a grimly depressing picture. We are choked and blinded by the filth we are dumping into our environments, and our plants and animals are endangered as well. We have already made sewers of the waterways—not to mention our contamination of the environment by the nuclear power plants that many people thought were the answer to all our woes. For there is the danger of long-lasting radioactive pollution in the event of leakage or more serious accidents. And thermal pollution by nuclear plants of some water is already a problem. Concerned scientists warn that our coastal waters may become "thick algae soups" in which fish and other useful marine life cannot live.

There is some truth in the warning that we are about to be buried in a mountain of solid waste, drowned in polluted seas, and choked by air we once thought was free to do with as we liked. Not forever can earth, air, and sea continue to be both home and cesspool at the same time. We must make some important decisions, and make them quite soon.

TOWARD A CLEAN WORLD

There are signs of what is ahead. Some of them are good; some are cause for serious concern. Let's consider the bad first, so that we can conclude this chapter on a hopeful note.

There remains a natural tendency on the part of most of us to look for someone else to blame. It is fashionable and satisfying just now to condemn mine operators and other heavy industry for creating our environmental woes. It is easy to point the finger of blame at jet aircraft leaving their smudgy trails across once-blue skies; to weep and complain about all the sea birds killed by oil or fish poisoned by chemicals flushed from a plant along the river. But we must shoulder our portion of the blame too. And we show reluctance about doing so.

In Phoenix, Arizona, in 1970 General Motors offered smog devices for older cars, installed for a price of only $20. Surely this was a small price to pay for cleaner air. Yet only one potential buyer in a thousand purchased the device! The other 999 either did not care about smog or were reluctant to spend money to fight it. In some states where smog devices are compulsory on new cars, it is fairly common practice to disconnect them on the sly, so there will be no "power loss."

If we will not take our own parts in the environmental fight, we cannot expect improvement. It is possible to control the mines and other large pollutors. But it will be vastly more difficult to police millions of individual citizens. We must ourselves decide to stop pollution.

There is real hope for the future in public attention to the sewage disposal problem. Public treatment plants have to be much more effective than those used in the past because of all the complex new chemicals that are now flushed down drains—phosphates and other washing compounds, new drugs and other chemicals, acids, weed killers, and pesticides. There are some 500 new chemicals marketed each year—so many that it is almost impossible for sanitation engineers to keep up with them all. Cleaning up waste water is a very expensive proposition, and cost is a big part of the reason for slow progress. Voters tend to turn thumbs down on outlays of money for municipal projects, even for new sewers. In spite of this, the United States has spent almost a billion dollars a year since 1952 to build about 7,500 new sewage-treatment plants.

At Lake Tahoe, a beautiful resort that was in danger of becoming dangerously polluted by increasing use as a septic tank, a modern three-stage 7½-million-gallon-a-day sewage disposal plant has been built. The resulting "effluent" is practically fit to drink before it is returned to the lake.

Several years ago the town of Santee, California, built a sewage disposal system that could well serve as a model for the rest of us. Processed sewage water is used to keep a pleasant lake filled for boating and fishing; there is even a swimming pool filled with this water. In other cities in the United States and elsewhere, sewage effluent is purchased after treatment for use as irrigation water or even reprocessed for domestic water.

America has had a Clean River and Harbors Act since 1895, but until recently the law had few teeth. In Europe the industrialized Ruhr Valley several years ago began to charge industries in proportion to the pollutants they put into the water. Factories paid for contaminating the water, in other words. With this economic incentive, many industries have gone ahead and cleaned up the waste water themselves before returning it to the common supply. We may come to this approach in our country.

Tough laws are now making it compulsory for industrial plants to install filters and cleaners. Dangerous chemicals are taken out of wastes sometimes to be used profitably, sometimes at a cost of doing business that must be passed on to the consumer. This is no more than right, for the time is past when we can treat air and water as expendable.

The fact that some effluents dumped into water can cause runaway marine growth is proof of their nutritive value. It has been suggested that with proper engineering and processing, sewage and other wastes can become valuable fertilizer for marine plants and animals and for land crops. Some waste materials are already being so used. The City of Muskegon, Michigan, is installing a sprinkler system over more than 10,000 acres to fertilize the ground by spraying thin city sewage effluent on it after solids have been removed. Here is the ideal solution to a pollution problem: turn the danger into something useful! Such an answer is not always possible, of course, and many such processes will be difficult and costly. The removal of sulfur from mine smelter smoke is an example. But since the alternative is far worse, it seems certain that the mines will find ways to better clean up the air they have used for centuries.

The present strong emphasis on pesticide dangers is having a beneficial effect on the situation. Under threat of a ban, chemical firms are producing safer materials; farmers are beginning to take longer and harder looks at the economics—and the even more important ecology—of pesticides. Much as we wish it, and although some newly christened ecologists might claim it to be true, the mess with which we have polluted our world these past centuries is not going to disappear by tomorrow with the wave of anyone's magic wand. But it is going to abate. There are already many hopeful signs. Lake Erie, Lake Michigan, and other ailing bodies of water, are being helped. Fish are still caught there. With tight controls to prohibit further fouling, nature can slowly begin to heal the wounds.

Pittsburgh long ago proved it was possible to clean up a dirty city. Los Angeles, once clean and sunshiny-bright, has at least brought its smog increase to a halt and now hopes to begin reducing the dirty brown pall that threatens Southern California. London, perhaps the dirtiest city for the longest time, has made miraculous progress with its Clean City legislation and is finding that it saves money in ways not even imagined before the cleanup took place. Birds and other wild life are coming back to London, and the people are beginning to find out what their historic landmarks look like under all that muck and grime.

Recently it was estimated that the cost of cleaning up the environment in the United States would be at least $71 billion during the first five years. While this sounds like a large amount of money, consider even $15 billion a year for five years, against our total current expenditures. The total would be only about 5 percent of our national budget and less than 2 percent of our Gross National Product. Surely it would be hard to find a better way to spend our dollars.

CHAPTER

9

Our Exploding Population

When Thomas Malthus wrote "An Essay on the Principle of Population As It Affects the Future Improvement of Society," there were only one billion people on earth. By 1970 there were more than 3.5 billion. Perhaps those billions are being better fed than the lesser number of Malthus's time, but this does not mean that his fears and bleak predictions of starvation were not well founded. There are reasons for his concern, and for the concern of many today who are involved in the problems of feeding all the world's people.

There were two key points in Malthus's arguments. First, there is a fixed amount of land on earth to be used for the growing of food, but the number of people to be fed is increasing all the time. Second, while the doubling of one billion to two billion posed no tragedy in the matter of food, the problem gets worse from there on, for as Malthus put it, billions are doubled just as quickly and easily as thousands.

Malthus was wise enough to know that improvements would be made in food production. But even assuming a 100 percent improvement each generation—a doubling of food—human reproduction increases far faster. He illustrated this very simply with two sets of numbers: 1,2,3,4,5,6,7,8,9. And 1,2,4,8,16,32,64,128,256. The first numbers represent the increase in food production, the second the increase in population.

For the first doubling there would be no problem, assuming that the land productivity would double too. But the next population doubling would result in four times as many people, and the increase in food would take care of only three times as many. From there on the situation would become worse with frightening rapidity.

Malthus used a doubling time of twenty-five years, since there were some areas in his time that were increasing at that speed, the United States included. In recent years the whole world population has approached the 25-year figure and presently is increasing at about 2 percent per year. At this rate of "compound interest" it will take only thirty-five years for the

If all a region's yearly income were divided equally among its people, each person would have the "average annual per capita income" shown on the chart. Of course, a few have more than the average and many have less. The average is useful for comparing the well-being of one region with another and for showing the typical income of an area. Graph by Population Reference Bureau, Inc.

ESTIMATED YEARLY PER CAPITA INCOME BY MAJOR AREAS OF THE WORLD, 1968

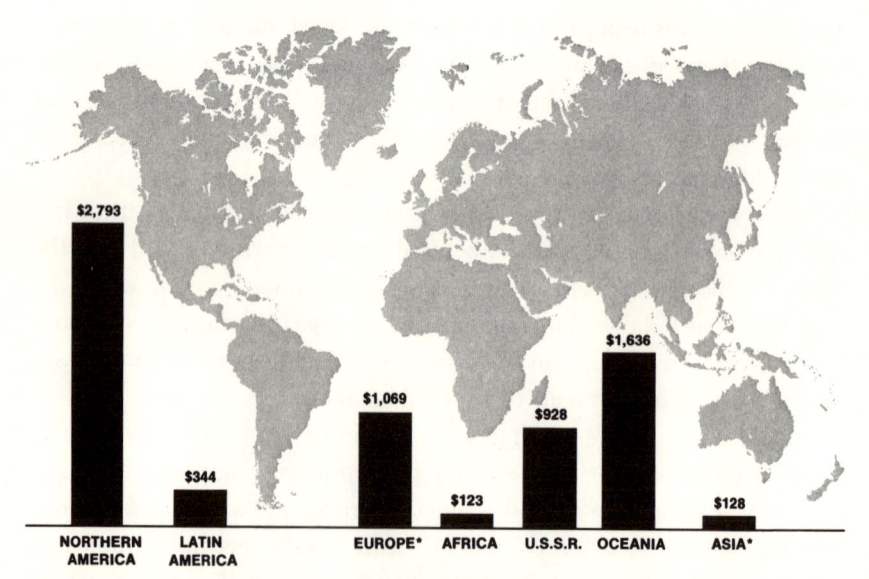

NORTHERN AMERICA	$2,793
LATIN AMERICA	$344
EUROPE*	$1,069
AFRICA	$123
U.S.S.R.	$928
OCEANIA	$1,636
ASIA*	$128

*Does not include U.S.S.R.

population to double. Soon after the year 2000 there will probably be 7 billion stomachs to be kept full instead of the 3.5 billion today. By about 2040 there may be 14 billion.

Today perhaps a third of the people in the world are at least hungry. Many are suffering from malnutrition. It is estimated that about 10,000 die every day as a result of improper nourishment. If the situation is so serious now, how much worse will it be in thirty years? In fifty years?

In Malthus's time it was possible to escape from population pressure and the food crisis by opening up new lands for food production or by emigrating to another land. Today that is becoming increasingly difficult. Australia is about the last of the new frontiers. It is easy to speak of farming new lands, but doing so requires great investments of capital, great new irrigation canals. In many areas new lands have proved to be worthless for agriculture anyhow, with soil turned almost into "pavement" by attempts at cultivation.

Even if we were able to double the amount of farmland on earth, that would be only a stopgap measure, for where would we go from there? Malthus was premature with his warning, but he was basically correct; the population explosion cannot continue unchecked unless we want starvation to step in and solve our problems.

THREE EXPLOSIONS

It is customary to represent the increasing human population as a curve that for most of man's time on earth has risen very slowly, but since about 1800 A.D. the number has begun to climb almost vertically. Actually there have been three distinct population explosions. The first occurred with the discovery of tools and weapons by man. In a relatively short period of time the population of humans jumped from about 1 million to 5 million.

Another explosion occurred with the agricultural revolution, with population surging upward from 5 million to 500 million in a few thousand years.

The scientific revolution has triggered the third explosion. Now the *geometric* power of population increase that worried Malthus is becoming evident. The old natural checks of starvation, disease, and wild animals have been drastically curbed; the power of human reproduction has been given almost free rein. The result has been likened to a spaceship leaving the launching pad. At first it moves upward ever so slowly, but gradually the pace quickens until it is racing away from earth at thousands of miles an hour.

We might also compare the population explosion with a chain letter, which declares that if its recipient will send out money to a specific recipient plus ten copies of the letter to friends, and if each friend who receives one will send out ten more, and so on down the chain, the recipient will be rich very soon. Chain letters seldom work for two reasons. First, people break the chain for one reason or another. And second, even if they do keep the letters going, there are soon no people left to write to. The geometry is 1, 10, 100, 1,000, and so on. On the other hand, the human chain is almost impossible to break. Two parents tend to have more than the "ideal" two children, and each of these children reproduces himself and then some. In a very few generations the earth will be overburdened with possible recipients of chain letters. That is, unless people voluntarily restrict the size of their families.

Ironically, the huge increase in population in recent years was caused by advances in science and medicine that have increased the life span. Today in the United States we can expect to live to slightly more than seventy years, on the average. Some foreign countries have an even higher life expectancy. Certainly this increased longevity—this chance to enjoy life on earth for far longer than our predecessors did—should be an unmixed blessing to mankind. But it also poses some difficult problems in food and population. Let's see why.

Prehistoric men lived, on an average, only about twenty-five years, it has been estimated from studies of skeletons from those times. Even during the Roman Empire life was very short. To assure that the race of men would go on, humans are able to reproduce at an age well below twenty-five. When the agricultural revolution made possible the scientific revolution and man began to lengthen his individual lifetime, the age of reproduction—the years of a "generation" of mankind—remained the same, for nature works very slowly in adapting man to changing conditions.

Two statistical rates determine the population. One is the birth rate; the other is the death rate. For hundreds of thousands of years the human birth rate remained quite stable at about 50 per thousand of population per year. This equals an increase of 5 percent. In early times the death rate approached the birth rate; in fact, in some areas it exceeded it and population actually decreased. There was only a slim margin of gain in "survival rate" until better medicine and sanitary conditions cut deeply into the death rate. Today there are countries with a death rate of only 6 per thousand. The rate is about 9 in the United States, and there are a dozen countries with lower rates. So what has happened? In simple arithmetic we have a much larger remainder when we subtract 6 from 50 than when we subtract 30 from 50. In some countries the increase will double the population in 18 years instead of 70!

While the population increase worldwide is 2 percent, it varies from country to country. In the United States it is only about 0.9 percent, an increase that requires more than 70 years for a doubling of population. In 1970 our birth rate stood at an all-time low of only about 18 per thousand, which is typical of the developed countries; Japan has a low increase, so do Germany and some other European countries. In general, as the death rate declines, the birth rate follows it down to balance population. But there is a lag of many years.

In the developed countries, death rates dropped over a long period of time. However, in recent years it has become possible for a country to acquire a low death rate almost overnight. In many Asian lands the death rate has dropped steeply since the end of World War II, but the birth rate has not yet declined.

In Iraq, where man may have first tilled the soil for food, the birth rate remains at 48 per thousand. But the death rate has dropped to 15, leaving a population increase of 3.3 percent a year. Should the death rate drop further, to 5, as it has in some countries, the population increase will then be 4.3 percent and will double in about sixteen years! Such an occurrence is not impossible. Kuwait, a small, oil-rich country on the Persian Gulf, in 1969 had a birth rate of 47 and a death rate of only 6, giving it an increase of more than 4 percent a year with its own population. Kuwait also had a great influx of immigrants to its rich oil fields and showed an increase totaling 8.3 percent, the highest in the world. At this rate, Kuwait would double its population in only nine years.

Europe is increasing at the rate of about 0.8 percent a year and will require about ninety years to double in population. Russia is increasing at only about one percent a year, as is North America. Canada is increasing at a slightly faster rate than the United States. Australia and New Zealand are increasing at the rate of 2 percent a year, which is not alarming considering their sparse present population and their great potential for feeding many more people.

It is in the other countries of the world, the so-called developing or undeveloped lands, that the greatest population problems exist. Africa is increasing at more than 2½ percent a year, Asia at just under 2½ percent. Latin American increase rates are even worse, about 3 percent a year. And these are the lands already feeling the pinch of hunger.

THE ABC'S OF ZPG

The concern over the alarming increase in population is not new. Benjamin Franklin wrote about the problem two centuries ago. Malthus is generally credited with defining the problem, and the population explosion is often termed the "Malthusian Nightmare." Many groups have for years advocated reducing the population growth to more manageable terms. Recently the President stated that some of our problems come from having added 100 million Americans to our population in only fifty years. Under these pressures, and for economic and other reasons, population increase in advanced countries generally has dropped to 1 percent or less. Even at this rate we will double our population by the middle of the next century, and the prospects of America with 500 million people is frightening, since we are already overcrowded in some areas.

Some groups urge the achievement of "Zero Population Growth" as quickly as possible. If we were to limit the size of our families to two children, it is estimated that growth could be checked by about the year 2020, at which time we would have about 250 million people.

Surprisingly, there are many who argue against curbing the growth of population. Some claim that only an expanding economy can be a healthy economy. Where would we be if we had limited ourselves to 100 million? it is asked. Surely there are 110 million Americans who would resent not being here to enjoy our country.

Another argument is that a stable population will naturally be an older population, with the average age moved up to 37 years from the 27 years it is at present. A "stagnation of ideas" is forecast, with a resultant stifling of youth in an older society. There is also fear of what might happen if we held

PER CAPITA INCOME AND POPULATION INCREASE OF SELECTED COUNTRIES, 1965

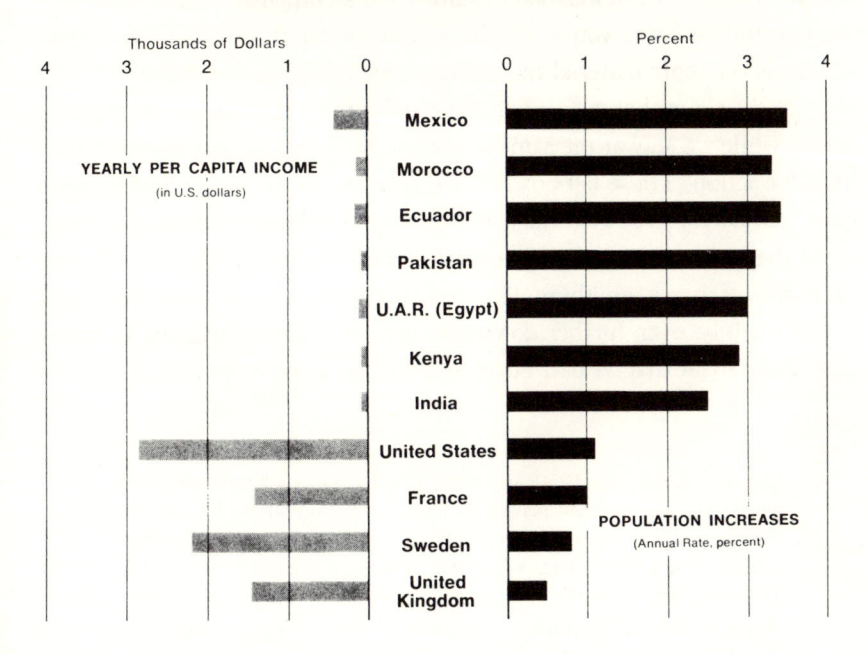

Rapid multiplication of people makes it difficult for the poor countries to raise per capita income. Note that the income figures per person are yearly, not monthly or weekly. A family of five in Pakistan, for example, would have a yearly income of $445. Graph by Population Reference Bureau, Inc.

our population to 250 million while other countries went on expanding at ever-increasing rates. Some argue that we might be overwhelmed by sheer numbers and not be able to cope with the rest of the world.

Answering the danger of insufficient food and other commodities, some advocates of large populations claim that if necessary the world could feed 50 billion people and more! Some scientific justification is available for such projections, and it might be technically possible to feed a world carpeted border to border and coast to coast with hungry humans. The proper question would seem to be not how many we can feed, but how many we should feed. Should we not be concerned with the quality of life as well as its quantity?

Most arguments against curbing population can be readily answered. Enlightened businessmen believe that a stable economy would be workable, and that it might even be more rewarding than the constant expansion we are faced with now. In answer to the charge that a stable society would hamper youth, with fewer opportunities and so on, it is equally true that there would be fewer young people to compete for those positions. There would also be more material and esthetic benefits for each of them.

To the claim that we cannot afford to let the rest of the world increase in size while we stay at the same size it can be answered that fear is a weak basis for action. Those nations that are growing fastest are underdeveloped ones that hardly pose a military threat to the developed nations. For many years they must exert all their efforts toward feeding themselves. By the time they achieve anything like technical competence, the developed nations will be even further down the road. It is hardly realistic to try to plan ahead so far that we don't even know what the rules may be.

Harvests during the 1950s in the developing nations barely outpaced population growth, and per capita food production showed a modest rise. Since 1963, however, population growth in these countries has continued at a steady pace while the increase in harvests has slowed. The numbers of malnourished people in Asia, Africa and Latin America are, as a tragic consequence, also growing. Graph by Population Reference Bureau, Inc.

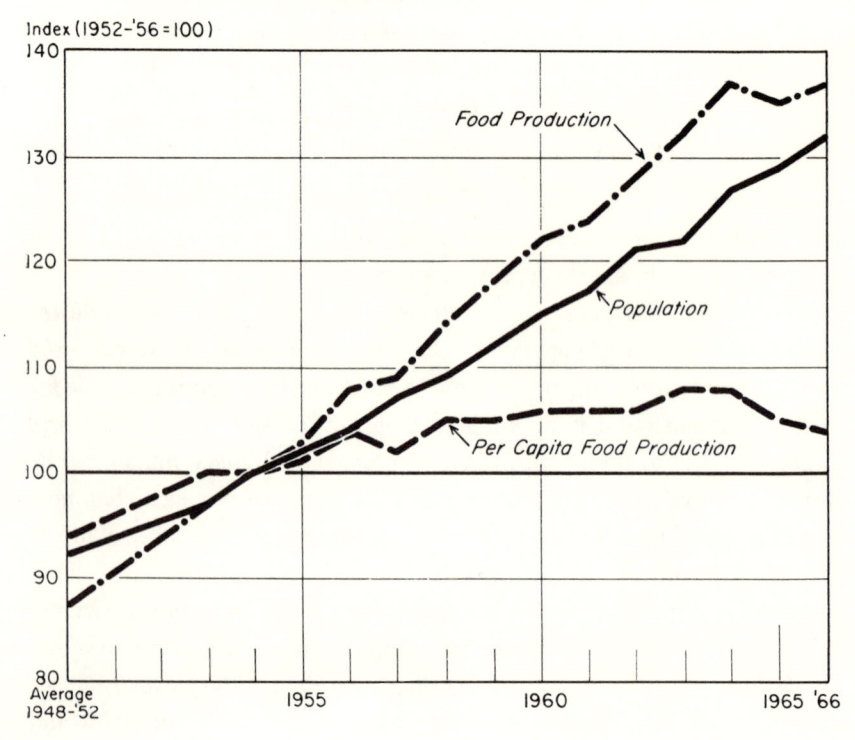

BUT STILL THE BABIES COME

There is one argument against population control that cannot be as successfully countered and that is the fact that most people want children because they love them, and very few parents have yet taken seriously the idea that we must control population. Our culture has been geared to a reverence for life and family, and children are largely what adults live for. It is difficult, if not impossible, cold-bloodedly to set aside this innate need for children to carry on as our "immortality."

It is very hard to convince the average parent today that a grave danger faces us if we don't quickly check population. Indeed, comparing life today with what it was when our population was half its size might even seem to argue for more people. The news that we are adding about 9 people a year for each 1,000 already here is not particularly alarming to most of us. At one time we were adding 30 to that number each year, and surely life is better now than then.

Even if we were to freeze population at its present level—which would be like trying to stop dead in its tracks a freight train moving at 100 miles an hour—this would solve none of our existing problems of overcrowding, crime, and so on. Can we ever return to the "good old days" that seem so dear to many? Some have said that we would be better off with 100 million people in the United States, but certainly no one advocates killing every other person to achieve this supposed ideal. And if this were done by some madman, could we continue to enjoy all the material things and services we have come to depend on?

Our nation's leaders have taken the problem most seriously. President Johnson appointed a committee of experts headed by John D. Rockefeller III, one of the most knowledgeable men in the field, to study the population problem. In 1969 that committee recommended a Population Commission, and that Commission is now functioning, with a goal of deciding on optimum population and working toward achieving it. Again, it will take a tremendous amount of education of our people to sell them on the idea.

Some decades ago our government sought by law to prohibit the drinking of alcoholic beverages. The idea of such a law can be defended, for surely alcohol is a great problem in our country. It kills ten of thousands of Americans each year, wrecks homes, and destroys lives. Yet the American people revolted at being told they could not indulge themselves in this way. They brazenly broke the law, and in the end the unwanted "prohibition" was removed.

Now, a love for children cannot by any stretch of the imagination be equated with a love for alcohol. Even if some people are convinced that in the long run having more than two children per family will harm our nation, it will still be difficult to convince individual parents that they should not have a child they want. And a law prohibiting the production of more than two children might be even less effective than the unenforceable Volstead Act.

The problem then, as usual, is people. People themselves must decide that population control will be for the best, just as people must, individually, decide that alcohol is harmful. There is encouraging evidence that the American people, as well as many other people, are at last beginning to realize that we cannot continue forever to increase our numbers. Somewhere there must be a size beyond which we should not—*must not*—go, for our own good and for the good of our descendants. John Stuart Mill spoke of the "greatest good for the greatest number," but we may have to adjust that definition. The "finest life for the optimum number" may be a better goal to set for ourselves and strive toward. But we will not do it by passing laws.

WHERE THE PEOPLE REALLY ARE

If it is a difficult problem to reduce population growth in countries such as ours, what of the developing or undeveloped countries? Advocates of birth control have worked diligently for half a century in lands like India, urging its people to have fewer children. If such efforts had succeeded they would have offset the reduction in death rates accomplished by medicine, sanitation, and better food. Yet India's current birth rate is 42 per thousand, and that of Pakistan is a frightening 50 per thousand. These developing countries have a population growth rate about three times what it is in the United States.

Again, it is difficult to point the finger of blame where having many children is traditional. In some countries with a high infant death rate it has always been necessary to have large families so that parents could be guaranteed a surviving son to care for them in old age. Long-standing traditions are not easily changed by well-meaning birth-control crusaders from England or America or Sweden. Trying to educate a population that is largely illiterate, and perhaps poverty-stricken as well, is a slow and patience-consuming process. In some countries plagued by hunger, spokesmen nevertheless cry out against those who recommend reducing the population, charging that these are attempts to wreck the developing lands by preventing their natural growth!

These are, of course, the lands that most need a reduction in population increase. There is an almost direct correlation between economic condition and population growth. Countries whose people have good incomes tend to grow more slowly. Population growth is fastest in countries that are poor—which unfortunately means that new citizens there will be even hungrier because they cannot afford food in either the quantity or quality they need.

There are some countries whose people average less than $100 a year in earnings, compared to the thousands of dollars per year per capita income in the developed countries. Even in some lands whose people earn far more than $100 it often takes a day's wages to buy one pound of meat! On a worldwide basis, 72 percent of the people have only 21 percent of the wealth, a most lopsided situation.

For some time many undeveloped lands have been attempting to increase their industrial production, believing that this would better their economic status. Unfortunately such attempts have generally failed. Nations that require most of their labor to produce food find it difficult to become industrial producers. The ratio of one farmer to 43 consumers that prevails in the United States is not typical worldwide, and in developing lands one farmer can feed only a few besides himself. Many people are "subsistence farmers"; that is, the whole family works on the land to produce just enough for them to eat. And many people who work at nonagricultural jobs spend most of their income on food, anyhow, so the result is about the same. Even in Russia, one of the great powers, consumers spend about half of their income on food and even then eat less than half the meat Americans eat.

Belatedly it has been realized that a nation must first become not only self-sufficient but efficiently productive in agriculture before it can be successful in industry. Then the process will begin to snowball. As more people are freed for other work than farming, more income is produced, which in turn provides incentives for farmers and a better diet for all concerned.

This Nigerian mother has learned that spoon-feeding instead of thumb-feeding of the newly weaned child not only is more hygienic but also aids the digestive process by using the baby's saliva. An Irish dietitian and a Dutch agronomist, FAO directed, introduced this church-sponsored Freedom from Hunger program. FAO Photo by C. Bavagnoli.

A student who has spent four years at the Santan Bailie School in China's Kansu Province stands beside a little coal miner "ant" just his age who has not had his dietary advantages. FAO Photo.

HUNGRY WORLD

Sadly, the alarming increase of population in the developing countries results in more and more mouths to feed through the same old-fashioned agricultural systems. If it is difficult to support 100 people on a given area of land, how can 200 live on that same amount? As population grows in the rural areas, and there is no opportunity for work, people tend to crowd into already overcrowded cities. One demographer has warned that by the year 2000 India may have *cities* with populations over 50 million!

In 1967 the United Nations formulated a declaration on the

population problem, signed by 30 nations who agreed that something must be done to check the explosion of humanity. This was no exercise in dramatics, for the world had just witnessed the frightening experience of crop failure in much of Asia in 1965 and 1966. India, Pakistan, and other countries faced widespread starvation, and it was necessary to send virtual gifts of millions of tons of wheat to save lives. An estimated 60 million Asians were fed with United States grain for two years, during which time our own surpluses fell dangerously low.

While this was a commendable effort on the part of our country and others that helped, it also showed that not for long can the few food-rich nations support the hungry world—especially if those overpopulated nations continue to add more millions to the load every year.

It is believed that thousands may die each day from starvation. Before we take some bleak hope from the fact that at least there will be more food for those left alive, consider that each day 200,000 people are added to the world's population as a *net gain* in excess of deaths. In one year more than 70 million join our ranks, and most of these millions are in the hungriest lands.

Most of us have been hungry at one time or another. Many of the world's unfortunates are hungry *all* the time. They have no problem with overweight; there is no fussing with a diet to help lose unwanted pounds. Starving children beg in the streets and eat scraps of garbage when they can find them.

There are two main types of starvation. *Marasmus* is the actual shortage of food, with not enough calories to keep one alive. This is outright starvation and, harsh as it sounds, perhaps brings the more merciful death of the two. For *kwashiorkor,* or protein-deficiency sickness, is a lingering death that may never kill but only cripple permanently. It is a disease that hits children when they are no longer fed milk and their new diet is lacking in proteins. Such victims are pathetic sights. One of the effects of hunger may be mental retardation in the young, a starving of brain cells such as has been observed in laboratory tests with undernourished mice. Coupled with this danger is another deficiency, the cultural deprivation that also takes its toll in development of the child.

Unquestionably population should be curbed in developing lands. To know this and do or say nothing about it would be inhuman to the point of being criminal. Yet it seems equally plain that the population will continue to increase the world over for several more decades at least. We have seen that in our country, for example, putting the brakes on right now would accomplish only a "sliding stop" in population growth that would skid us all the way to the year 2020. Most authorities are convinced that despite continuing efforts and modest success with population control, we can expect as many as 7 billion people on earth by the year 2000.

To deny that we have a population explosion is not to face facts. A little over three hundred years ago, after hundreds of thousands of years, there were only half a billion people on earth. By 1850 the next half billion brought the total to one billion, a nice round number. Compare the speed of increase: In just 200 years man matched the growth of the preceding 700,000 years or more! And in less than 80 years he had again doubled his numbers, this time to two billion. The next doubling will occur by 1975 when there will be four billions on earth. The view ahead takes on the frightening aspects of the story of the Sorcerer's Apprentice, who having turned on the water forgot how to make it stop.

We won't drown in a sea of humanity, of course. But that sea of humanity itself may well starve to death, an even more horrible fate, if something does not happen to change the population curve. Dr. René Dubos uses a term more fitting than "explosion" for the population phenomenon we are witnessing. He prefers to call it the population "avalanche," picturing a pile of humanity snowballing downhill, gathering both mass and momentum as it goes—more and more biomass increasing at an ever-accelerating rate.

One way or another, the number of humans on earth will be limited. Every irresistible force must some day meet its immovable obstacle, and the productivity of earth will be the ultimate check. It would seem far wiser to forestall such a catastrophic solution voluntarily by setting sensible limits on population. Such a goal may be the most important challenge ahead for our young people.

Even if population could be frozen at 3.5 billion we would still need more to feed that number *properly*. Men of good will are presently engaged in a mighty effort to spread the use of improved seed varieties that have caused a "green revolution" in India, Taiwan and some other developing nations. Despite these advances, unless there is an enormous increase in food production, there will be famines that will make the worst ones in history look like rehearsals.

CHAPTER
10

To Feed the World

In 1965 and 1966 a long siege of bad weather hurt the food crops in Asia, causing disastrous shortages. However, since that time the "green revolution" in agriculture, consisting of miracle grains, mechanization, chemical treatment of soil, and biological and technological know-how, has more than kept pace with population growth. Barring some unforeseen problems, there seems to be no further setback in store for the developing countries with respect to food if they can keep their birth rate in check. Continuing aid toward self-sufficiency for the hungry world is being given by the developed countries, and must continue to be given as long as necessary. Feeding the the world is an effort that is truly global in scope.

THE "INDICATIVE WORLD PLAN"

The United Nations Food and Agriculture Organization in 1970 published its "Indicative World Plan for Agricultural Development." Begun in 1963, at the first World Food Congress, held in Washington, D.C., this "IWP" plan extends to the year 1985. Subtitled "A Strategy for Plenty," the Plan is concerned mainly with the developing countries in what the United Nations calls Zone C. Zone A, the developed countries of

Plenary Hall during the 15th session of the FAO Conference in Rome in 1969. The United Nations organization proves that a pooling of experience can allay the world's most pressing problems and benefit all. FAO Photo.

North America, Europe and Oceania, and some others, are considered capable of feeding themselves with present programs. Zone B, the Communist countries, are classed as "centrally planned," and taking care of their own problems. Zone C, then, includes Latin America, Africa, Asia, and the Far East. The approximately 1.4 billion people in it represent 44 percent of the world's population.

It is difficult for most of us to appreciate the problems faced by those in the developing lands, accustomed as we are to plenty of food and other necessities plus many luxuries as well. In the less fortunate countries, 7 people of each 10 depend on agriculture for their livelihood, and their annual income is shockingly low, even allowing for different currency values. Rural Africans, for example, average $43 per year! Asians do little better at $46. Highest on the scale are those in rural Latin America who average $138 a year. The meaning of "subsistence farming" becomes clearer, for it is plain that these few dollars will not buy much in the way of supplemental foods after other necessities have been met. Because of primitive methods and low productivity per farm worker, these 70 percent of the population produce only about 30 percent of their countries' wealth.

The IWP study shows that by 1985 the demand for food in the developing countries, or the "Third World," as it is often called, will be almost 2½ times as much as it was in 1962, the base year for the plan. Discouragingly, the increase from 1962 to 1969, if continued for the time until 1985, would produce less than double the amount of food. This would result in great shortages and the need to import $40 billion in food for 1985. Since the developing countries spent only $3 billion on such imports in 1962, there is little chance that they will be able to afford more than thirteen times that sum in 1985. The solution is increasing the rate of food production in their own countries. IWP lists five key objectives in reaching this goal (emphasis has been added):

1. Securing the staple food supplies, with population growing at 2.5 to 3 percent per year. For most countries this means a faster growth of *cereal* production.
2. Improving the *quality* of the diet. This calls for adjusting to the changes in the composition of the diet that accompany rising incomes and urbanization, and to specific requirements in food policy that emerge from the analysis of the main dietary deficiencies. Here the supply of *protein, particularly animal protein,* is the crucial problem.
3. Earning and saving the foreign exchange that is crucial to financing overall development. Emphasis must be upon both *boosting exports* of agricultural products and *reducing imports* through economic substitution.
4. Providing a large part of the additional employment that will be needed over the period up to 1985, and at the same time helping to create *jobs in industries related to agriculture.*
5. Increasing productivity through *intensified use of the physical resources* of land and water, including forests, oceans and inland waters.

Since cereal grains, such as rice and wheat, are the main sources of calories and protein in human diet and also necessary for feeding livestock, IWP recommends accelerated production of these cereals. Helping to achieve this goal are the "miracle" rices and wheats that have already demonstrated their ability greatly to increase yield per acre.

A second, and more difficult, goal is that of providing the right kinds of foods to combat malnutrition. In the developed countries the calories consumed daily averaged about 3,000 in 1962, while the developing lands

An FAO-trained home economics educator in Malawi holds a display of protein foods. She is part of the national community development program, which mobilizes adults to raise standards of living and education. FAO Photo by F. Botts.

Below: Peace Corps volunteers from Massachusetts, Illinois and Iowa visit "Porky," one of the star boarders at the Animal Reproduction Center in Loja, Equador, with Dr. Adolf Faller (right), an Equadorian veterarinarian. Peace Corps Photo by Vernon K. Richey.

averaged only 2,200. Even allowing an extra 250 calories for those of us in developed lands because the climate is generally colder and we are generally larger people, there remains a "calorie deficit" or "hunger gap" of about 500 calories. The picture becomes somewhat brighter when we recall that we are generally overfed about 15 percent; the actual calorie deficit in developing countries is about 6 percent or 150 calories per day of perpetual food shortage.

However, the situation is worse with respect to protein. In 1962 we in the developed countries averaged 85 grams of protein daily, more than half of it in the form of high-quality animal protein. The developing countries provided only 57 grams, of which 11 percent was animal protein. Our protein intake in the United States is almost double that of Asians, and we get nine times as much animal protein!

IWP therefore recommends the accelerated production of hogs and poultry in the developing lands, since these animals yield food much more quickly than do slower-growing cattle. Poultry mature within weeks, and hogs within months, compared with the years required for beef. It is not suggested that beef production be slowed, however, since it too must increase to provide sufficient meat.

IWP foresees a need for 69 million tons of fish a year for food by 1985, plus 38 million tons more for fish meal for animal feed. This total of 107 million tons is about 80 percent more than the current catch and requires the expenditure of an estimated $8.5 billion of capital for more modern fishing equipment.

"Intensive use" of natural resources will include wide-scale irrigation projects and extensive and intensive use of fertilizers. With help from the developed countries many developing lands are now building fertilizer plants. If meat production is to be increased, fertilizer must be used even on grasslands and pasture. The extent to which fertilizer use is expected to increase is shown in projected costs. While 1962 expenditures totaled only $664 million, 1985 will require $7.8 *billion!*

The total dollar amount estimated to carry the Indicative World Plan through the year 1985 is $110 billion. This is a huge sum of money and will undoubtedly require loans on an international basis. More importantly, it will require a realization on the part of developing countries that agriculture is a business and that food sufficiency will come only through efficient business methods. Part of the requirement is that there be incentives for farmers to produce large quantities of crops from their fields. With land reform in many countries there will be a growth of "cooperatives" formed among local farmers for more efficient production, distribution, and marketing of their products. As they require less effort to feed themselves, the developing countries will be able to produce more for export, thus realizing a profit that can be used to better their living standards, including the importing of foods not locally available.

If the Plan is successful, agricultural production in the developing lands should increase by 3.6 percent a year until 1975 (compared with only 2.7 percent yearly from 1962 to 1969) and by 3.9 percent per year for the final ten years.

The village of Tura, in Kenya, is a distribution point for vitaminized soup brought by the Red Cross, the only nourishing food these people are getting since disease killed off the cattle that are their usual food source. FAO Photo by P. Pitter.

BEYOND IWP

Most authorities are hopeful and optimistic about the prospects for world food through 1985 and even to the year 2000. The FAO some years ago predicted that protein output would rise steadily until the year 1990, increasing the daily rations of the developing countries. But what of the time after that, when it seems that we may have caught up with the limits of food production by conventional methods?

There are of course those who feel that even conventional agriculture can feed far more than the 6 or 7 billion who will populate the earth in 2000. Reputable scientists have estimated maximums of 40 to 50 billions, and even in excess of 100 billion if we settle for bare subsistence diets. For other than nutritional reasons, it is strongly to be hoped that we never find out if the the world can indeed support thirty human beings for every one now alive. However, if the need arises, there are food production methods on the drawing board—and some already in pilot plant stages—that promise great increases in productivity and efficiency, although some of them hardly sound appetizing to consumers accustomed to steaks, great varieties of succulent vegetables, and gourmet delicacies and desserts.

Many of our breakfast foods, flours, and other products are "fortified." This means that additional quantities of protein and vitamins and minerals have been added. Protein-rich products such as "Incaparina" are made of cereal and cottonseed flours, with lysine added for extra protein. "Fortifex" adds methionine to cereal and soy flours. FPC, or "Fish Protein Concentrate," is another example of high-protein additive that enriches or fortifies flour or other foods.

While some 11 million tons of soybean, coconut, peanut and other oilseed plants are used every year, there remains about 70 million tons of oilseed meal that is wasted to human nutrition. This contains up to 50 percent of good-quality protein. But instead of being fed to humans it is used as animal feed, or even as fertilizer, for which latter use it is poor.

Much research and some practical work has been done toward using this great supply of protein. Among the products developed in addition to Incaparina and Fortifex are "Multi-Purpose Food," and "Laubina," the last a very successful food developed in Lebanon.

It has been suggested that starch produced cheaply in potatoes and other root crops might be a source of food for yeast-growing organisms.

Using starch in a more direct way, researchers in Great Britain have converted potatoes, yams, and sugar into a high-quality protein said to be comparable to that of milk. Britain's National Research Development Corporation is so pleased with results of a pilot plant that produces 100 pounds of powdered protein a week that it has granted $1,200,000 for the building of a full-scale factory to convert starch into protein.

The marine plant algae is another potential food source. This rapidly growing organism is available in a wide range of types, from giant seaweeds to single-celled plants of the kind that plague our swimming pools and ponds in warm weather. Experiments with the algae *Chlorella* indicate very high yields per acre, and the Japanese have commercially produced small amounts of this protein-rich stuff. It is, however, rather expensive and is hardly ideal as to taste and even digestibility.

Green leaves are also a source of protein. For some years experimenters at England's Rothamsted Station for agricultural research have extracted a protein concentrate from leaves. Like algae, it suffers from taste problems. However, both these sources show promise, and there are lots of algae and green leaves in the world!

One research project is currently investigating the possibility of reclaiming cellulose waste from the city dump for use as animal feed. It is estimated that for every person in our country there are about three pounds

Open-air culture of algae, showing turbulence in the culture caused by bubbling air through it. FAO Photo.

of such trash disposed of every day. If the huge logistics problems of reclaiming this material can be overcome, here is a source of some 100 million tons of potential animal feed, from which we might produce about 10 million tons of meat or milk. And that would be about 100 pounds of high-protein food for each of us.

HYDROPONICS—THE PLASTIC FARM

There is a good possibility that many of us who don't yet know what hydroponic farming is have already eaten and enjoyed the crops such agriculture produces. Tomatoes, cucumbers, chard, and some other vegetables—and even grass for feeding animals—are now being produced on a commercial basis in a number of hydroponic facilities around the world.

Several centuries old in concept, hydroponics began to become a factor in agriculture during World War II when barren islands were able to produce vegetables for military men stationed on them. Basically such facilities are the old familiar greenhouse, or hothouse, used to produce food rather than plants and flowers. Growing in gravel beds rather than in a farm field, and in a plastic-enclosed, artificially heated or artificially cooled environment (perhaps with additional carbon dioxide pumped into it) rather than in the open air, hydroponically grown plants are not subject to drought, flood, windstorm, or attack by insects. Man himself is the only "pest," and hygienic measures are taken so that he will not infect his plants.

With the advantages mentioned, hydroponics grows several times the quantity of crops per given area produced by conventional agriculture. While it is difficult to imagine a huge alfalfa field under plastic, or a Kansas wheatfield completely enclosed, the day may be coming. At present a number of small facilities produce several hundreds of grasses daily, grown from seed in about seven days.

With no pesticide costs, and chemicals metered and delivered right to the roots through special plumbing, and far less water wasted inside the enclosed environment, plastic farming may be the agriculture of the future.

TISSUE CULTURE

As far beyond hydroponics as that practice is from old-fashioned dirt farming is "tissue culture." This is not a brand-new idea, either, and the noted Dr. Alexis Carrel astonished the scientific world in the 1930s by growing bits of animal tissue, including his famous chicken heart, as laboratory cultures. Supplied with nutrients, much as fertilizers and water are fed to plants, these bits of living animal cells continued to live and even to grow.

Research continues in this promising field, and there is some culture

The benefit of a plastic mulch is demonstrated in a U.S. experimental plot. U.S. Department of Agriculture Photo. *Below:* 4-H Club members in Korea are learning the technique of using vinyl houses for growing early vegetables. FAO Photo.

of tissue for medical purposes. Predictions are made of some day being able to grow whole organs for replacement in ailing humans—hearts and kidneys, for example.

Tissue culture is defined as "the branch of biology in which tissues or cells of higher animals and plants are grown artificially in a controlled environment." "Cell farming" takes place in vessels filled with nutrients, and there is the possibility of establishing "banks" of various tissues so grown.

Recently some research was done on the growing of food in this manner. Tomato cell tissue, for example, might be grown in laboratory containers. Only the meat portion of the tomato would be cultivated—no skin, stems, vine or roots. Animal tissue like eggs and meat could be cultivated in the same way—pork chops with no bones, for example, and vegetables conveniently shaped for packaging and use.

Under certain conditions, plant tissues produce "undifferentiated tissue"; that is, a mass of cells that continue to grow and produce larger and larger amounts. This mass can be cut into smaller pieces, and each piece will grow in a nutrient environment.

Tissue culture is a refinement of hydroponics, since it eliminates the unwanted portions of a plant. In the culture production of meat, bone, gristle, pinfeathers, and so on would not be reproduced. Perhaps flavor would not, either!

FOOD FROM OIL

Petroleum is a hydrocarbon; that is, it is composed of carbon and hydrogen. It is not just a coincidence that this sounds similar to carbohydrates, for petroleum is an organic material formed from the bodies of tiny organisms over ages of time, just as coal is organic and produced from vegetation in much the same way. The idea of eating oil or coal does not sound appealing, yet food is being produced from both!

It has been known for some time that certain bacteria feed on oil; in fact the bugs pose a serious problem in aircraft fuels, since they sometimes clog the fuel lines and so must be dealt with in the interests of safety. Several years ago a German biologist raised bacteria on oil, and French scientists at a petroleum laboratory became interested. In the years since then, they and other workers in many countries have grown yeasts using petroleum as food for the microorganisms. The idea is far more promising than it sounds.

Yeast reproduces by "budding," a process tremendously faster than plant or animal growth. Yeast doubles its weight in hours, rather than weeks, months, or years as is the case with plants and animals. And the efficiency of conversion of oil into yeast is high; about 50 percent on a production basis, and much higher in some experiments.

While the yeast product is not suitable for direct human consumption, it is used to feed animals, and these are in turn eaten by man. In taste tests with pork, consumers were unable to tell which pig was raised on conventional foods and which one had eaten yeast grown on oil.

There are a number of strong arguments in favor of this kind of food production. A refinery is even less subject to flood, drought, or storm than a hydroponics farm. Pests are no problem, and production is not seasonal. There are refineries all over the world, and prices of petroleum are quite stable. And it is estimated that a very small percentage of the world's

Mobil Oil Corporation scientists at Princeton Laboratory show protein powder on the left (equivalent to 1.2 pounds of steak), made from the amount of petroleum shown in the beaker on the right. FAO Photo.

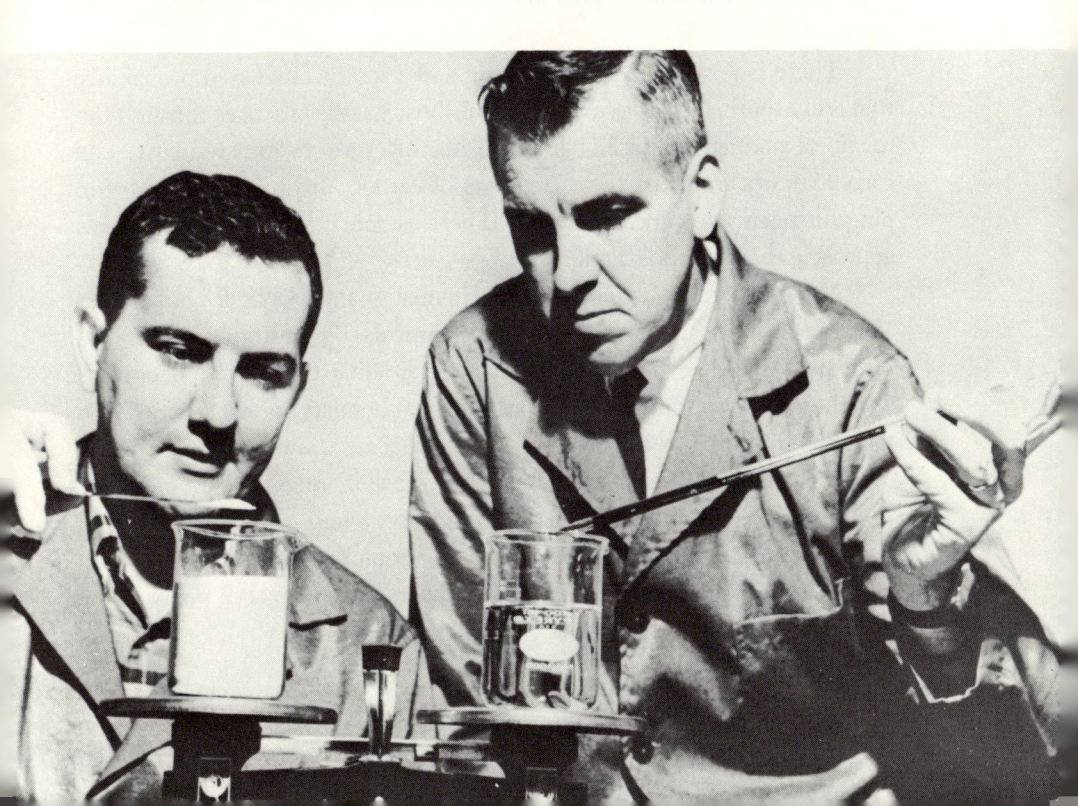

production of oil could provide our protein needs. To the argument that this could compete with other uses for petroleum, it can be answered that nuclear power plants are beginning to phase in and may lessen the demand for petroleum as a fuel.

There is also one very strong reason why petroleum does not now, and probably will not for many decades, feed the world's people—or at least its meat animals: Such food is simply not needed as yet. When and if it is, the petroleum industry should be ready to start turning out fuel for hogs and cattle rather than for automobiles.

SYNTHETIC FOODS

A fairly standard item in science-fiction is the menu of "food pills," a steak compressed into an aspirin-sized tablet, or the nourishment of freshly baked potatoes squeezed into something just as small. For good physiological reasons—not to mention some powerful psychological ones—we won't be getting our nourishment from such food pills for some time, if ever. Much less than half of our present old-fashioned food is waste, and much of that "waste" is in the form of roughage necessary to continued good digestion. A diet of food pills will work only if we are willing to eat about as much weight in pills and water as we now eat in conventional foods.

There is a much more interesting and scientifically based probability that truly synthetic foods could supplant those nature produces through the magic of photosynthesis. This is the manufacture of fats, proteins, and carbohydrates from the basic elements of carbon, hydrogen, and oxygen plus nitrogen and other nutrients. There is much more science to this approach than there is fiction.

Many years ago a German chemist named Friedrich Wöhler "manufactured" urea from inorganic chemicals. Up until that time it had been supposed that there was a solid wall dividing the organic chemicals and those that were inorganic. In fact, many chemists argued strongly and for some time that Wöhler was mistaken, that he could not possibly have synthesized urea. But he had done just that, and since his time man has synthesized many biochemicals, including proteins.

There was a time when man relied on agriculture for most of his cloth and building materials. Today synthetic fibers have displaced many of the old-fashioned naturally made fibers. There are also inorganic compounds that serve as building materials in place of wood. Rubber and many dyes were once available only as plant substances but now are largely made synthetically. The synthesis of food is a similar process, and there would be many advantages in producing food in this way instead of on the farm.

Growing cotton requires a huge amount of land, good weather, rain or other water supply, fertilizer, pesticides, plus work involved in planting, weeding, irrigating, and picking. Making such synthetic fibers as nylon also involves raw materials, equipment, energy, manpower, and so on, but there are far fewer variables involved. The chemical factory can be programmed to turn out a certain product, and it will do that within very close tolerances. There is a great deal of automation in such industry, and the people working in it are generally paid higher salaries than farm laborers. There are no pink bollworms or disastrous floods. The chemical plant can operate around the clock all year long without regard to sun or season.

Presently available as animal feed, for a cost of about fifteen cents per pound in large quantities, there is a hydrocarbon product called 1-3 butanediol. Although it is not suitable for human food, because of its bitter taste, among other reasons, butanediol is an example of the possibilities of using simple chemicals as food. In time suitable synthetic carbohydrates may be developed, along with synthetic fats to supplement the carbohydrates and proteins.

The same benefits would be available in a plant producing synthetic foods. "Yields" could be tailored exactly to demand; different products could be produced quickly as needed. Instead of vegetables low in lysine or methionine it would be possible to blend ideally nutritious foods in whatever consistency, texture, color, flavor and appearance are desired. No energy or raw materials would be wasted in producing stalks, leaves, or other inedible parts. Instead of incurring the 90 percent loss of the "law of tithes" common in the production of meat and animal products, a pound of raw material would produce practically a pound of food. Quality control would be very easy, and again there would be no need for pesticides or the other bothersome requirements of "old-fashioned" food production methods. Where transportation for long distances was necessary, the blended materials could be more easily shipped minus the water that makes up most of the weight of all foods.

To lay to rest any fears that such artificial foods would not be tasty, there are now on the market what are called food "analogs" or copies, actually "spun" into fibers and made into "meats" and other foods that find excellent acceptance as everything from dog food or steaks for dinner. Interestingly the food fibers are spun as "monofilaments," or single threads, just as are nylon, dacron and other synthetic textiles.

These analog foods are not true synthetics, since they are spun from a natural food source such as soy bean protein. They also use such raw materials as oilseed from cotton cake, peanuts, sesame seeds, or sunflower seeds. Presently much of this oilseed is wasted after the oil and cotton fiber are used. Protein from oilseed meal costs from 8 to 12 cents a pound, compared with about 65 cents for milk protein and $1 to $2 for meat protein.

SPACE FOOD

Our astronauts have reached the moon and in doing so have spent weeks away from the earth in the closed environment of spacecraft. However, they have not produced their own food as they went along but carried along enough at the start. What of long trips, say a trip to Mars and return, that would require a year or more? Because each man will need 1½ pounds of food, 2 pounds of oxygen, and 5 pounds of water per day, a year's trip would require more than 1½ *tons* of supplies per man. With six men aboard, the weight would increase to 10 tons. Understandably, space planners are designing life support systems that are tiny copies of earth's ecology.

In such a "closed-ecology" spacecraft system, the raw materials of carbon, hydrogen, oxygen and nutrients would be recycled over and over just as we do on earth, on a much larger though not quite so obvious scale. Instead of taking along 10 tons of food, air, and water, perhaps one-tenth this amount might do. Liquid and solid wastes would be processed for reuse, with nutrients extracted from them to help grow additional food, just as is done on earth. All that would be required would be a source of energy—the sun, or possibly nuclear energy.

For years algae was the favorite space food of the planners. It converts perhaps 20 percent of the solar into food energy, quite an efficient rate of

The spaceman's meal in the plastic packages is equivalent in food value to the luscious meal on the plates. The water gun (left) is used by astronauts to reconstitute some of the freeze-dried food. Bite-sized dehydrated food can be eaten directly from the package.

(Below) A technician in a Gemini Capsule at the Whirlpool Corporation in St. Joe, Michigan, demonstrates how a spaceman drinks orange juice. (Photographs courtesy National Aeronautics and Space Administration.)

conversion. However, it is now thought that keeping sunlight focused on the algae "farm" might be too much of a problem, with all the other requirements of space missions. Much thought has been given to using hydrogen-eating bacteria such as those that produce food from petroleum. Fed on urea and CO_2, these tiny workers produce carbohydrates, fats, and protein but no oxygen. The water they do produce would have to be broken down by hydrolysis into oxygen and hydrogen. While this system does not need sunlight, energy would have to be taken along in additional hydrogen, which would add somewhat to the weight of the payload. Engineers estimate that a closed environment with about thirty quarts of liquid per man would be sufficient to provide him with food and air. It would also take about one kilowatt of power to operate the system for each man using it.

Such a diet would be very high in protein, and NASA considers supplementing it with some fats and carbohydrates produced synthetically, perhaps from formaldehyde.

When man begins to set up bases on the moon and the planets as well, the question of food will arise even more importantly. Since solar energy is available everywhere in the solar system, hydroponics may make it possible to grow food even on barren and airless planets by keeping the "farm" enclosed in plastic. It is quite likely that there will be beneficial scientific and technical fallout for earthbound agriculture and food production from such efforts. For now, however, all we have to show are some high-energy beverages and "space food sticks" that are more novelty than real nutritional accomplishment.

The fuel cell, which mixes oxygen and hydrogen to produce electric power, also provides a byproduct in the form of water that is suitable for drinking. Here, on the microcosm scale of spacecraft ecology, is an example of how the power cycle and life cycle can be linked to the astronaut's benefit.

Man is an ingenious creature, and he has an inquisitiveness that leads to all sorts of new discoveries and different methods for getting things done. There are a variety of other ways we may feed ourselves in the future, ranging from farming the sea by herding fish the way we now do cattle, and killing off the marine predators that compete with us for seafood, to growing crops in salty irrigation water.

There are wild animals we could eat in more abundance, such as rabbits and kangaroos, although such meat is admittedly as springy as it is stringy. Authorities have recommended using other even more interesting animals, such as the eland, a large African antelope said to be very tasty and available in abundance. Also the dugong and manatee, plant-eating marine mammals that do not compete with us or our meat animals for food, and the capybara, an aquatic rodent which is nevertheless said to be good meat for human diets.

We may never have to go to these alternatives to hunger; on the other hand we may use them all. If we ever exhaust them all, clever humans may figure out other sources of food. But we had best not depend on that!

Index

abomasum, 35
acorns, 83
adenosine triphosphate, 40
adipose tissue, 45
agricultural revolution, 70-86
Agriculture Department, U.S., 49, 112
air pollution, 114-115
albuminous substances, 47
algae, as food, 145
alimentary canal, 36
amino acids, 13, 39; essential and nonessential, 48; protein and, 47
Amitschow, 7
animal husbandry, 96-101
animal products, 62-64
animal protein, meat and, 68-69; need for, 56; world supply of, 140-142
anorexia, 8
antrum, 34
appestat, 8
apple orchards, pesticide problem in, 111-112
arachidonic fatty acids, 44
Arcimboldo, Giuseppe, 11
arteries, hardening of, 6
Aswan High Dam, Egypt, 96
atherosclerosis, 6-7

ATP (adenosine triphosphate), 40
aurochs, 60
automobile pollution, 114

bacteria, hydrogen-eating, 154; in stomach, 34
barley, 80
Barr, W., 1
beef production, 96-97
beri-beri, 53
beverages, 83-86
biological oxygen demand (BOD), 116
biology, in farming, 88-91
biotin, 55
birth control, 128-130
blackstrap molasses, 13
body, as "furnace," 30
body fat, 46
bolus, 33
bongo fish, 67
Bos primigenius, 60, 96
Boussingault, Jean, 90
Braconnot, Henri, 47
Braidwood, Robert J., 72
bread wheat, 80
Breughel, Pieter, 4
butter, 62-63

Index • 157

cachexia, 46
caloric intake, recommended level of, 10
calorie, 3; kinds of, 42-43
cannibalism, 60
canning, 102-104
capillaries, 39
carbohydrates, 39; calories in, 43; digestion of, 35; proteins and, 13; solar energy and, 25; sugars as, 43
carbon dioxide, 16; discovery of, 30
Carrel, Alexis, 147
cassava, 49, 81-82
cattle, ancestors of, 60; ecology and, 25; as food, 58
cells, food delivery to, 38-39
cereal grains, 71
cereals, 78-80
cheese, 62-63; atherosclerosis and, 7
chemical preservatives, 104
chemical sprays, 108
Chlorella, 145
chlorophyll, 29
cholesterol, 37
chyle, 38
chyme, 35, 38
clams, 67
Clean River and Harbors Act, 121
clean world, steps toward, 120-122
closed-ecology system, 152
clupeoid fish, 66
cocoa beans, 85
coffee, 85
colon, 37
Columbus, Christopher, 76, 85, 91
combine, harvesting, 95
commensalism, 21
competition, 21
condiments, 86
corn, 71; hybrid, 91; parched, 73
corpus, 34
cows, stomach of, 35; *see also* cattle
crop improvement, 76-78
crop rotation, 89

Darwin, Charles, 76
DDT (dichlorodiphenyltrichloroethane), 108-111, 115
deficiency diseases, 52
deglutition, 33
demersal fish, 66
diet, age, caloric intake and proteins in, 56; foods and regimens in, 4, 10-14
digestion, 32-33
disaccharides, 43
die
diseases, deficiency, 52; high-fat diet and, 6-7
Donora, Pa., fog, 115
drugs, dieting and, 11
duodenum, 36

eating, pleasure in, 10-11; weight problems and, 4-6, 10-11
ecology, food chain and, 21; "law of tithes" in, 24; life cycle and, 23
eggs, 61, 96
einkorn wheat, 79
emmer, 80
energy, from food, 29-41
environment, "law of tithes" in, 24-27
enzymes, in digestion, 32-33; protein breakdown by, 41
epiglottis, 33
epithelial cells, 38
Erasistratus, 30
erosion, ecology and, 113
esophagus, 33
esters, 44
eutrophication, 116
exercise, 10

Faller, Adolf, 141
FAO, *see* United Nations Food and Agriculture Organization
farm engineers, 91-95
farming, biology in, 88-91; early history of, 71-76; hydroponic, 146, 154
fat(s), calories in, 43; in cells, 39; cholesterol and, 7; diseases associated with eating of, 6-7; increased consumption of, 46; overeating of, 6; types of, 44
"fatted calf," 57
fatty acids, 44
fish, 64-68; atherosclerosis and, 7; killing of by pollutants, 116-117; water pollutants and, 116; world needs of, 142
fishing, electronic aids to, 100
Fish Protein Concentrate, 68, 144
folic acid, 55
food, canning of, 102-104; chemical

preservation of, 104; cooking of, 73-74; delivery to body cells, 38-39; digestion of, 32-33; distribution of, 104-106; energy and, 29-41; freezing of, 102; as human fuel, 1; as largest industry, 87-106; "manufacture" of, 15; need for, 1-14; obesity and, 4-6; from ocean, 20, 25-27, 65-67; from petroleum, 148-150; population and, 123-124, 133; problems of, 4-5; protein-fortified, 144; pyramid of, 22-24; smoking of, 102-103; sun drying of, 102; synthetic, 150-152; in Third World, 139; wild animals as, 27-28
food analogs, 152
Food and Drug Administration, U.S., 44-45, 48-49, 84, 108-109, 134, 138-140
Food and Agriculture Organization, *see* United Nations Food and Agriculture Organization
food chain, 15-28
food concentrates, 104-105, 144
Food for Peace Program, 102
food industry, 87-106
food pills, 150
food preservation, 101-105
food production, per capita yearly average, 19
foodstuffs, basic, 42-56
food supply, population and, 123-124, 133
food web, 22
Fortifex, 144
fowl, as food, 61-64
Franklin, Benjamin, 21
Freedom from Hunger Campaign, 109, 134
freezer-trawlers, in fishing industry, 101
fructoses, 43
fruits, 83; sun-drying of, 102
fuel cell, 154
Funk, Casimir, 51-52

Galen, 2-3
gasoline, heat energy in, 3
"gas sylvestre," 30
Gemini capsule, 153
Genesis, 57, 71-72
ghee, 63
glucose, 41, 43

gluttony, 4
glycine, 47
gram-calorie, 3
Grand Banks, Newfoundland, 100
grasses, wild, 77
green plants, 16
gullet, 33

Haber, Fritz, 26, 90
harrow, 93, 94, 95
harvesting combine, 92, 95
health foods, 13
heat energy, 3
Helmont, Jan Baptista van, 15, 30
heterosis, 91
high-fat diet, diseases associated with, 6-7
Hippocrates, 1-2, 29
hunger, food production and, 87; *see also* starvation
hunger pangs, 8
hybrid corn, 91
hydrochloric acid, 34, 41
hydroponics, 146, 154
hypothalamus, 8

ileum, 36
Incaparina, 144
income, population growth and, 129
India, population growth in, 132, 135
Indicative World Plan for Agricultural Development, 138; objectives of, 140; world protein needs and, 142
industrial pollutants, 113-116
inorganic pollutants, 115-116
insect pests, 89; "birth control" for, 112
intestines, 36-37
irrigation, 76-77
Isabella, Columbus and, 91
IWP, *see* Indicative World Plan for Agricultural Development

jejenum, 36
Johnson, Lyndon B., 131

kilocalorie, 3, 42
kwashiorkor, 136

Lake Erie, 122
Lake Michigan, 122
lakes, restoration of, 122

Lake Tahoe, 120-121
lamb, 60
Lamb, Charles, 73
lampreys, larval, 26
Langworthy, C. F., 50-51
Laubina, 144
Lavoisier, Antoine, 30-32
law of tithes, agriculture and, 70; meat production and, 68
leucine, 47
Liebig, Justus von, 47, 90
life, as chemical function, 32
life cycle, plants and animals in, 23
life span, changes in, 126
light, food energy and, 18-19; *see also* sun
"Limeys," 52
Lind, James, 52
linoleic fatty acids, 44
linolenic fatty acids, 44
lipase, 35-36
lipids, 44
locust plagues, 88
"long pig," 60
lysine, 91

macronutrients, 90
McCollum, Verner, 52, 56
McCormick, Cyrus, 93
Macquer, Pierre, 47
Malthus, Thomas, 87, 123-124
maltose, 36
man, as hunter, 58-59
Mangelsdorf, Paul, 80
marasmus, 136
Markham, Edwin, 91
Masai warriors, 58
meat, cost of, 68-69; in diet, 12-13; as luxury food, 57-69; as protein, 25, 68; U.S. consumption of, 97; vital need for, 69
mercury poisoning, 113
metabolism, 30; enzymes and, 41
micronutrients, 50, 90
microvilli, 38
milk, as basic dairy product, 62; protein in, 49, 69; water content of, 64
milkfish, 67
Mill, John Stuart, 132
Millet, Jean François, 91
minerals, 50-51

mine smoke, 113, 121
miracle wheat, 91
Mobile Oil Corporation, 149
monosaccharides, 37, 43
monounsaturates, 44
mucus, function of, 34
Mulder, Gerardus, 47
Multi-Purpose Food, 144
muscle, 40
mutton, 60

National Academy of Sciences, 10, 42, 56
National Aeronautics and Space Administration, 153-154
National Research Council, 42, 56
National Research Development Corporation, 145
net protein utilization, 49
niacin, 53, 55
nitrogen, in food chain, 17, 20
NPU (net protein utilization), 49
nutrition, 10-14; laws of, 50-55

oats, 80
obesity, death from, 5-6
oceans, food from, 20, 25-27, 65-67
Ohio River, pollution of, 115
oil spills, 118
olive oil, 7
omasum, 35
organic pollutants, 115-116
osmosis, 38
overeating, 4-5; cause of, 8
overweight problems, 4; death and, 5-6; remedy for, 10-11
oxygen, discovery of, 30
oysters, 67

Pakistan, population growth in, 132
pantothenic acid, 55
paprika, 54
parasites, crop damage from, 21-23
parched corn, 73
Peace Corps, 141
pelagic fish, 66
pellagra, 53
peptones, 36
peristalsis, 33, 35
pesticides, as pollutants, 108; water

pollution and, 115
pet food, 20
petroleum, food from, 148-150
pharynx, 33
photosynthesis, 16-17, 41; efficiency of, 18-19; solar energy and, 18
phytoplankton, 25
plankton, in life cycle, 25-27
plants, agricultural revolution and, 71; animals and, 23; chemical needs of, 89; danger to from parasites, 22-23; energy stored in, 18; fish and, 67
plastic farm, 146
plows, 75, 95
pollutants, organic and inorganic, 115-116
pollution, 107-119
Polo, Marco, 90
polypeptides, 36
polysaccharides, 43
polyunsaturates, 7, 44
Ponderosa pine disease, 114
population, determinants of, 126-127; in developing lands, 136; food and, 133; in India and Pakistan, 132; per capita income and, 129; world growth in, 136
population explosion, 20, 123-137; three stages in, 125-128
pork, 60
potatoes, 81
poultry, as food, 61-64; production of, 96
predation, 21
prehistoric man, life span of, 126
Priestley, Joseph, 30
Prohibition era, 131
protein, 46-50; absorption of, 46; animal, 25, 56, 68-69; amino acids and, 47; body weight and, 50; calories in, 43, 46; carbohydrates and, 13; enzyme breakdown by, 41; meat as, 25, 68; muscle as, 40; net utilization of, 49; starvation and, 136; world supply of, 140-141
protein-fortified foods, 144
proteosis, 36
ptyalin, in digestion, 32

reaper, 93-95
rennet, 62

respiration, process of, 31
reticulum, 35
rice, 71, 80, 91
rivers, pollution of, 115-118
Rockefeller, John D. III, 131
Rothamsted agricultural research station, England, 145
Royal Navy, 52
rumen, 35

saccharin, 81
safflower, 45
salivary amylase, 32
Sanctorius, Santorio, 30
scurvy, 52
seafood, 64-68
seasonings, 83-86
seaweed, 25
sewage disposal, improvements in, 120-121
shaduf, 77
Shanidar Cave, Iraq, 59
Shaw, George Bernard, 11-12
sheepherders, 59-60
shellfish, 67
smelter fumes, ecology and, 113
smog, 114-115, 120
smoking, as food preservative, 102-103
soil, food production and, 15; tilling of, 74-76
solar energy, 15-18, 29, 154
soybeans, 13
space food, 152-155
spoon feeding, 134
starches, 43
starvation, death from, 6; gluttony and, 4; types of, 136
steapsin, 36
Stefansson, Vilhjalmur, 13
stomach, of cow, 35; growling of, 37; peristalsis in, 35; structure and function of, 33-36
sugar, as carbohydrate, 43; as energy food, 44
sugar cane, 81
sun, carbohydrates and, 29; food and, 15-16; plant growth and, 18
sun-drying, of food, 102
supermarket, in food distribution, 105-106
sweet potatoes, 81
symbiosis, 21

synthetic foods, 150-152
Szent-Gyorgi, Albert, 54

tea, 85
texture mung protein (TMP), 9
Third World, food demand in, 139-140
Tiber River, pollution of, 117
tissue culture, 146-148
TMP (texture mung protein), 9
tongue, 32
trachea, 33
tractors, in mechanized farming, 94, 95
tree crops, 83
trypsin, 36
tyrosine, 47

United Nations, Food and Agriculture Organization, 9, 49, 65, 77, 82, 84, 88, 109, 117, 134-135, 141, 143, 145, 147, 149; Indicative World Plan for Agricultural Development, 138-155; world population and, 135-136

vedalia beetle, 112
vegetables, 80-83
vegetarianism, 12
villi, 38
vitamins, 51-56; consumption of, 55; fat-soluble, 46; source and purpose of, 55; A, 46, 53-55; B, 55; B_{12}, 55; C, 53, 55; E, 46, 54-55; K, 46, 54, 55

Warburg, Otto, 18
waste pollution, 114
water, eutrophication of, 116; as mineral, 51; in plant food cycle, 16-17; pollution of, 114-118
weight, loss of, 10; excess, 4-6, 10-11
whales, 66-67
wheat, bearded, 92; einkorn, 79; emmer, 80; miracle, 91; use in bread, 80
wheat germ, 13
Whirlpool Corporation, 153
wild animals, as food, 27, 154-155
wild grain, 74
Wöhler, Friedrich, 150
world food plan, 138-155
World Health Organization, 110

"X disease," of Ponderosa pine, 114

yams, 81
yeast, petroleum and, 148-149
yogurt, 13

Zawi Chemi Shanidar, Iraq, 59
Zero Population Growth, 128-130
zooplankton, 25

HD
9000.5
.H34
1971

HD
9000.
.H34

1971

$5.00

FEAST and FAMINE

By the author of

MAN ALIVE
NINE ROADS TO TOMORROW
HABITAT
BEYOND TOMORROW
SCIENCE AND SERENDIPITY
CENTURY 21